CROWDED CANVAS

To John,

With thanks for

good memories.

As ever,

Rod

Rod was a student at
Queen's Collyc
Birmingham

CROWDED CANVAS

Faith in the making

ROD GARNER

Scripture quotations, unless stated otherwise, are from the New Revised Standard Version of the Bible (Anglicized Edition) © 1989, 1995 by the Division of Christian Education of the National Council of the Churches of Christ in the United States of America. Used by permission. All rights reserved.

ISBN 978–1–905958–23–8

First published by Inspire
4 John Wesley Road
Werrington
Peterborough PE4 6ZP

Typeset by Regent Typesetting, London
Printed and bound in Great Britain by
Printondemand-worldwide.com, Peterborough

For John and Carol Lang
with thanks and gratitude

'How can we combine the old worlds in new orders so that they survive, so that they create beauty, so that they tell the truth?'
Virginia Woolf

Contents

Foreword

Provoked by Richard Dawkins' *The God Delusion*, not to mention other trends in the perception of religion in our culture, a priest and pastor here counters negativity about faith by giving personal testimony to the rich life of mind and heart fostered by the Christian tradition – thus demonstrating that the picture of faith offered by atheist and fundamentalist alike is a travesty of the real thing. This alternative picture is entitled, *Crowded Canvas* – for, indeed, that is what we are pointed to. Written out of fascination in order to fascinate, this book draws from the whole range of things that give faith depth and richness, creating a collage from poetry and philosophy, science and saints, holiness and history, creation and community, music and meditation, theology and tragedy, literature and life.

This, then, is no conventional apology, nor is it a systematic theological exposition of Christian faith. Rather from anecdote to Augustine and Aquinas, not to mention Scripture and pastoral experience, we are led into a depth of meaning and commitment which issues in greater assurance, as well as a profound silence before the workings of providence and the signs of the kingdom. The reality of death is faced, and the elusiveness of goodness. The wealth of wisdom from a huge range of reading material is particularly welcome in an age where experience and the internet easily marginalize books. I commend this stimulating read to anyone who seeks an understanding of what faith means for intelligent Christian believers.

Revd Frances Young
Emeritus Professor of Theology,
University of Birmingham

Introduction

In search of inspiration to help me with this introduction I went to my trusted friend the dictionary to see what it had to say about faith. No surprises really: 'strong or unshakeable belief in something esp. without proof; trust in God, in his actions and promises; complete confidence in a person, remedy etc.'. Satisfied but not sufficiently intrigued I allowed my eye to roam a little to the entry above faith and there I noted, with a wry smile, the word fairy-tale. The definition included 'highly improbable, fabrication, fantasy, cock-and-bull story, fiction, invention'. My hunch is that quite a lot of people just now would prefer to see faith listed under fairy-tale on the grounds that it represents an untruth bolstered by tall tales that lead to unhappy or dismal endings. Richard Dawkins' *The God Delusion* has proved a massive bestseller, and on both sides of the Atlantic a good deal of polemical writing has faith in its sights. For the first time, to my knowledge, atheism has its own section in leading American bookstores and a recent poll by a national British newspaper revealed that a majority of those interviewed thought that religion did more harm than good. Since leaving office, former Prime Minister Tony Blair has also noted, with some exasperation, how influential figures who voice religious opinions run the risk of being caricatured as 'nutters'. Not the most elegant description perhaps, but it does confirm that when faith asserts itself in the contemporary public square it can expect to face alarming ignorance or hostility.

How should we react to this? By 'we' I mean my prospective readers, those who already stand within communities of faith or are at least prepared to give faith a fairer hearing than some of its shrill and ill-informed detractors. It is worth recalling that faith has always had its 'cultured despisers', those who find religious claims improbable, offensive or immoral. Christianity therefore faces a perennial challenge to speak compassionately, persuasively and reasonably to those who think differently. This calls for hard thought and the humility which recognizes that our critics are sometimes right. Faith can display a mean and vicious demeanour that runs counter to the claims of Christian charity. For this we can only plead 'Lord, have mercy' and resolve to do better. This means being able to demonstrate that faith is a good, generous and life-giving thing – rich in its appreciation of what it means to be human, responsive to the needs and questions of these anxious and confused times and truthful in its claims and demands.

This book, in part at least, is a personal and, I hope, considered response to these challenges. I want to celebrate faith as a deep and authentic way of living that goes beyond simplicities and embraces struggle and questions without any questionable need to be always right. The following chapters draw heavily on my experiences of my life and my work as a priest, pastor and theologian. To some extent they show how I have come to faith in God and what I think it means to hold on to Christ as a source of grace and truth. They attempt to be honest and presume that faith shrivels unless it is fed by prayer, silence, a scriptural word and the medicine of the sacraments. More than this, however, they invite the reader to travel hopefully, to take risks and to retain the curiosity and imagination of the child. Faith invites us to look everywhere for traces of the divine, to live as much as we can and to face honestly what we sometimes fear or shirk. If, at one level, faith represents an invitation to 'travel in' as part of the search for personal identity, it is also a summons to explore and cherish our world. As the title of the book makes clear, I have come to see faith and, for that matter, life as a 'crowded canvas'. There is a fair amount of theology in these pages but there is also history, politics, philosophy, personalities, books and music, travel and conversation. I cannot imagine my life or my religion without such riches and shall be happy if my enthusiasms encourage others to find fresh paths to the waterfall.

Thanks, as always, are due to former parish administrator, Ruby Smith. A lesser woman might have issued legal writs against me by now, such is the state of my handwriting! She continues, however, with great patience and skill to decipher and process manuscripts that need much concentration before they yield their treasures! I am also deeply grateful to the American friends, pastors and scholars whose kindness and generosity have made recent trips so stimulating and enjoyable. In particular, I must record a debt to John and Carol Lang whose help, hospitality and humour are fondly remembered. This is also a good moment to thank the students and congregations in a variety of locations who have helped to fashion this book through their love of questions and the engaging desire to understand more fully what they profess or would like to believe. I remain in debt to my nearest and dearest: a 'crowded canvas' sometimes entails that loved ones take second place. For their forbearance and love: thank you to Christine, Daniel and George.

Rod Garner
April 2008

1

Other People's Trades:
The Fascination of Things

In my early twenties I had a brief encounter with Bertrand Russell, arguably the most widely read (if not the best) British philosopher of the twentieth century. I carried his books to work, absorbing his ideas before the warmth of the train carriage lulled me to sleep, and I was moved by his passions – the quest for love and understanding and a professed concern for the ills of humanity. My mind was being formed and Russell spoke with magisterial authority on life's mysteries. Many years later I would learn that his altruism was marred by unattractive personal traits and his knowledge of things was less than assured. In a celebrated letter to *The Times* Valerie Eliot wrote:

> Sir,
>
> My husband, T.S. Eliot, loved to recount how late one evening he stopped a taxi. As he got in the driver said 'You're T.S. Eliot.' When asked how he knew, he replied 'Ah, I've got an eye for a celebrity. Only the other evening I picked up Bertrand Russell and I said to him "Well, Lord Russell, what's it all about?" and, do you know, he couldn't tell me.'[1]

The letter ends there and we are left contemplating the scene – the eminent thinker momentarily dumbstruck, and the frustrated cab driver still waiting for a reply. I warm to Russell in this instance: to ask 'What's it all about?' is to introduce into any conversation a tangle of vague assumptions and ideas concerning the *givenness* of the world and its possible meanings. In an uncharacteristic moment of intellectual humility, perhaps the distinguished philosopher recognized the wisdom of silence in the face of the most fundamental of questions that innocently disarms all those who come with easy answers or theories that encapsulate everything. Religion fails to compel when it claims too much, and science and philosophy alike appear desultory and mean when they assume the omniscience that former times attributed only to God. Reading Richard Dawkins' latest polemic against religion,[2] I am struck by two things: firstly, his engaging admission that we inhabit a tantalizingly complex world that clearly enthrals him and, secondly, his belief that ultimately all this complexity – including everything that presently eludes our conceptual grasp – will be rendered intelligible by the human mind. He is aware that some respectable voices within the scientific community hold that the universe is 'not only queerer than we suppose but queerer than we can suppose'[3] but regards this as a faint-hearted doctrine, ill-suited to the inexorable scientific mission to reveal and make plain everything that is presently concealed.

This naive presumption that what we are able to grasp with our five senses is all the reality there is seems out of joint with our understanding of a world replete not only with atoms and molecules but fantastically large amounts of dark matter or energy that elude our powers of observation and rationality. It is also far removed from the perennial philosophy of East and West which has always claimed that the flux and order of things find their ultimate explanation in a transcendent reality. And in the shared experiences of many people of all faiths or none, it fails to do justice to the well-documented conviction that certain moments instil in us an unshakeable belief that *there must be more than this.*[4] Such revelations or disclosures invariably induce a sense of awe and humility and in the presence of 'otherness' we find ourselves drawn irresistibly to what Rudolf Otto described as *mysterium tremendum et fascinans.*[5] The fascination lies in the fact that we cannot help ourselves, that unexpectedly in a bewildering variety of ways we become acquainted (if only briefly) with the beauty that lies at the heart of things and imbues the turning world with unimagined depth and significance.

About the time that Bertrand Russell came into my life, I took myself off to see America, travelling alone coast to coast, courtesy of the Greyhound bus system. I was armed with a notebook, an overnight bag, the poetry of William Blake and a hunger for new experience. So it proved. I still have the log of my travels and the memories of those remarkable weeks journeying from 'sea to shining sea' remain indelible. Blake helped me to look and see in a fresh way and a changing vista of breathtaking grandeur overwhelmed me. But another fascination was born on that journey out of an awareness that seemingly inconsequential events were no less significant than the silence of the Grand Canyon or the Eden-like innocence of a great National Park. The delight of hot water and clean sheets after long, tiring rides; the taste of coffee and cake and the pleasure of conversation in roadside cafés where local citizens would ask me (ask me!) what life was like in the big American cities I had seen; the stately procession of the Staten Island Ferry in no way diminished by the towering Manhattan skyline; the crisp, clean air of a late October morning and an unexpected stroll down a main street with a friendly stranger intrigued by an English accent. I returned to England ready for new work but also more receptive than before to the notion that common life and small things can bear a transcendent splendour and that 'even a walk to the mailbox is a precious experience'.[6]

In the intervening period of more than 30 years I have become increasingly convinced that faith is sustained and nurtured by a fascination with a world that surprises us at every turn. Our readiness to be amazed and our *receptivity* to what is going on around us really do matter in the long walk of faith that calls us to become sons and daughters of God. In the sublime prologue of John's Gospel, the evangelist records that Jesus 'came to what was his own, and his own people did not accept him (1.11). But he then goes on to say that to 'all who received him . . . he gave power to become children of God' (1.12). There is much to meditate on here, not least the startling notion that grace and truth wait upon us – wait upon our response and receptivity before we can turn to the true light that contains our salvation (1.9). My contention is that, Damascus road experiences apart, we become children of light when we glimpse its radiance not only in the face of Christ but in the wonderful 'nowness' of everything and the awesome complexity of the world.

Concerning 'nowness', the art lies in the recognition that life can only be defined in the present tense:

it is and it is now. At funeral services I occasionally use the lovely words of Joyce Grenfell: 'There is no such thing as time, only this minute; and I am in it, thank the Lord.' Each minute an occasion for gratitude, each hour an opportunity to give our attention to the incipient joys and latent possibilities of this day. As for complexity the sheer profligacy and strangeness of life becomes evident the moment we allow ourselves to be addressed by the world. In my reading of the life of Charles Darwin, two events have fixed themselves in my memory apart from his argument that species progress from the simple to the complex over hundreds of thousands of years. One is the tragic death of his little daughter Annie – an event so personally devastating for Darwin that it was to colour in darkest hue his growing doubts concerning the providential ordering of a world in which such things could happen.[7] The other, in a quite different vein, is the pleasing image of Charles, ever the intrepid explorer, returning triumphant from an afternoon of insect collecting and noting with great delight and satisfaction that he has recorded a catch of more than 50 types of beetle. It looks impressive until we know the facts.

The famous British biologist, J.B. Haldane, was once asked to give his opinion on God. His reply, 'He is inordinately fond of beetles', seems to fit naturally alongside Darwin's successful afternoon excursion. Currently there are at least 350,000 catalogued species with new forms continually being discovered. They can fly, swim and survive being swallowed by a predator by digging their way out through its body. Their instincts were formed 100 million years ago and they will eat anything, living, dead or decomposed. Their armour has evolved a resistance to impact, chemical agents and radiation. In the event of some far-reaching nuclear catastrophe, they would emerge intact from their underground shelters a metre deep as our successors. They inhabit our world but nothing ties us to them. In Kafka's famous story 'Metamorphosis',[8] the travelling salesman, Gregor, wakes up one morning from disturbed sleep to find that he has changed into an enormous beetle, so large and unprepossessing that his family can no longer stand his presence. I am neither for nor against beetles as such, and given Gregor's sudden grotesque transformation, the response of his family is entirely understandable if somewhat harsh. But I am amazed by the dexterity and imagination of beetles, by their ability to adapt and survive and their stupendous variety. To paraphrase Darwin, there is a grandeur in such a strange world of teeming and ingenious activity but not even the author of *The Origin of Species* could have been aware of the even stranger mysteries of the deep oceans that cover 70 per cent of the Earth's surface. Only now are we beginning to realize that the deep sea, as the largest of all habitats, is home to an extraordinary diversity of organisms. Along with colossal squid and sinister dragon fish that fire beams of red illumination from lamps under their eyes, there are to be found creeping sea lilies, snails with armour-plated feet and photosynthetic bacteria thriving in hydro-thermal vents where the water is hotter than 121^0 C.[9] Entire ecosystems exist at pressures that alter biochemistry and exotic creatures move silently through our seas, in shapes and forms that we normally associate with the stuff of dreams or the more fabulous achievement of the human imagination. The new world of underwater exploration is bringing to our television screens dimensions of our planet that constitute a different kind of buried treasure – gold and jewels, so to speak, that just happen to be there, not to be appropriated or collected for selfish human ends and not apparently fulfilling any grand purpose in what we vaguely call the wider scheme of things. The surprise and delight that we feel as these fantastic forms of life are paraded before us may be connected with an intuitive awareness that their point and value lie precisely in the fact that functionally they have nothing to do and nothing to prove. They just *are*, in all their randomness and contingency, being themselves as part of a baffling created order where beetles are apparently loved by God.

This nature trail is taking us in two directions and both lead us away from a commonplace understanding of the world and the popular image of the Great Architect of the Universe that holds it in being. A religious view of things extends beyond what is normally regarded as pleasing or even beautiful and faith can find in complexity fascinating and unexpected sources of revelation. I want to bring St Augustine in here to strengthen my argument. Too often he is misunderstood or caricatured as a theological polemicist or a joyless Christian thinker with no capacity for pleasure or delight. In fact, as both *The Confessions* and the *City of God* reveal, Augustine has a keen sense of both the order and the unexpectedness of the world. He can revel in the 'abundance of light and its miraculous loveliness, the dark shades of woods and the multitudinous varieties of birds with their song and bright plumage'.[10] But he is also fascinated by other people's trades: the waiter at Carthage who serves him roast peacock that manages to stay fresh and edible a year later; the goldsmiths and jewellers that trade in precious stones and diamonds with remarkable properties that we fail to register because 'daily familiarity gradually blunts the edge of wonder';[11] the people who can swallow various articles without harm or sweat when they choose. He is even aware of individuals who 'can produce at will such musical sounds from their behind that they seem to be singing'.[12] The miracle of fire also intrigues him along with the force of magnetism and the apples of Sodom that disintegrate into dust and ashes when bitten. We are also told of the man down at the harbour with feet shaped like a crescent and only two toes on each, and another man recently born in the East with two heads and four arms.[13] Such freaks may serve only as amusement or a source of derision to other onlookers but for Augustine they pose questions: how could they be derived from Noah who was a perfectly normal man, and what is their purpose in a world that is 'a marvel greater and more wonderful than all the wonders with which it is filled?'[14] Complacency of any kind is alien to Augustine: he is forever thinking in questions, pushing and probing as his fertile mind oscillates between strange observable phenomena and the unknown region that is the habitation of God. What connections can be made between the creation and the creator and what if anything does the former reveal to us of the latter?

This greatest thinker of the early Christian centuries is challenging us at this point to move beyond the familiar paths of piety that find God exclusively in Jesus, blue skies and golden sunsets and venture tentatively along the road less travelled in order to encounter the imagination and power of God as the 'Maker of heaven and earth' – the first statement, we may recall, of the Creed. Indirectly, and I offer this suggestion with some caution, he is also inviting us to regain a balance in our faith that sometimes appears in danger of losing the mystery of God through an excessive preoccupation with the person of Christ, the assurance of sins forgiven and the sure knowledge of his love for us. It may prove to be the case as Karl Barth has argued that the name of Jesus is the final and definitive word that makes sense of an ambiguous world but, in the perplexing interim that characterizes our lives, we are to remember that the doctrine of creation takes precedence over the saving work of Jesus precisely because, as Sara Maitland has expressed it:

> In the beginning God created.
> In the beginning God created heaven and earth.
> In the beginning God created heaven and earth
> and saw that it was good.
> Before God redeemed, God made.[15]

Repeated slowly and deliberately the verse can take root in us and is worth learning by heart. It has the quality of a mantra pointing us back to the opening chapter of Genesis and its insistence that matter is good and that making rather than rescuing is what God is fundamentally about. The inherent fascination of the verse only becomes evident when we realize, firstly, that creating is a continuing activity of God. In the prayer of General Thanksgiving[16] we bless God for our 'creation, preservation and all the blessings of this life'. But as we do so are we aware that creation and preservation constitute one and the same thing? Without the energy of God coursing through us and everything that lives we would not be: to paraphrase the Psalmist 'it is he that made us and we are his (Ps. 100.3). Secondly, the more we reflect on the incredible diversity of a world that is manifestly odd, in some ways peculiar and still largely unknowable, the more it seems we are required to sit lightly to a notion of God as the cosmic artificer ordering and shaping every last detail of nature. What emerges in its place is something more risky and provocative: a flamboyant, ebullient and profligate God shedding forth a universe so intricate yet so random that our words trail off in silence and we suffer the 'poverty of speech' that Augustine knew only too well as he contemplated the diffuse materials of his Maker.

Although she might blush at the comparison, Annie Dillard displays in her writing a fascination with the natural order that effortlessly brings Augustine to mind. Her book *Pilgrim at Tinker Creek*[17] is a detailed and highly personal account of what Blake would have described as the 'minute particulars' in the ever changing panorama of the Shenandoah Valley in Vermont. Tinker Creek appears to her as

> an active mystery, fresh every minute. It contains the mystery of the continuous creation and all that providence implies; the uncertainty of vision, the horror of the fixed, the disillusion of the present, the intricacy of beauty, the pressures of fecundity, the elusiveness of the free, and the flawed nature of perfection. The mountains are a passive mystery, the oldest of all. Theirs is the one simple mystery of creation from nothing, of matter itself, anything at all, the given.[18]

She sees with a clear, almost detached eye, never succumbing for a moment to the dubious impulse to interpret everything as a form of benediction. She acknowledges the predatory dimension of the landscape – the tooth and claw that feeds on weaker things – but

alongside this she is also captivated by the creativity
of God:

> Look at practically anything – the coot's
> feet, the mantis' face, a banana, the human
> ear – and see that not only did the creator
> create everything, but that he is apt to cre-
> ate *anything*. He'll stop at nothing. There
> is no one standing over evolution with a
> blue pencil to say, 'Now that one there is
> absolutely ridiculous and I won't have it'. If
> the creature makes it, it gets a stet. Is our
> taste so much better than the creator's? The
> creator creates. Does he stoop, does he speak,
> does he rave, succour, prevail? Maybe. But
> he creates. He creates everything and any-
> thing.[19]

We are back to beetles, the skulking dragon fish of
the deep and disorderliness that asks to be accepted
as an inexorable element of the way things are, along
with the palpable line of beauty that still falls short
of perfection. There is order and flux, precision and
randomness, a dependability that does not disappoint
us – the sun rises as it always has – and, equally en-
thralling, an inherent playfulness in the universe that
is tantalizing and revelatory if we can rid ourselves of
the manacles that still hold us to a mechanistic understanding of how things are. I like the story of the
girl brought up in a family with a strong devotional
attachment to the Virgin Mary. As a very small child
she misheard the words of the *Ave Maria*: instead
of 'Holy Mary, Mother of God, pray for us sinners
now and at the hour of our death', she thought the
petition ended 'Holy Mary, Mother of God, *play*
with us sinners now and at the hour of our death'. A

delightful recollection and a serendipitous mishearing that induced within the growing child a sense of joy and connectedness brought about by the realization that she could feel at home in the universe. Her daily prayers presented the creation as God's playground with the mother of Jesus lending a carefree and spontaneous hand.

I recognize that this story will not persuade the cynic or the sceptic. The eminent Oxford Physical Chemist, Peter Atkins, whose disdain for Christianity is marginally less than the vituperative writings of Richard Dawkins, has argued against the existence of God on the grounds that if God did actually exist God would stand accused of being lazy or careless given how much has been left to chance within the ordering of things. I find the argument unconvincing and will explain why shortly. For now I want us to stay with the emerging picture of God that is more akin to that of the artist rather than the engineer or architect: a high-energy, high-wire God, taking risks, flinging stars into space and, even more precariously, assuming flesh and entering a created order that ultimately was not amused by the playful child of Nazareth who, becoming a man, invited his followers to risk everything for the sake of the kingdom. As we know, the invitation was declined and the multitude turned against him. The poet Edwin Muir, in his fine poem 'The Killing',[20] places himself amongst the mocking crowd and as a stranger notes that he 'could not read this people or this outlandish deity'. According to the dictionary 'outlandish' means 'strange, odd, bizarre'. Nowhere else in my reading have I come across such an epithet attached to the crucified Jesus and it reveals in a shocking way the otherness of Christ and the furious resistance to his message.

There is, I believe, a pattern here disclosed both in the indeterminacy and unscripted dimensions of living – the way the world of matter actually is – and the God who, far from gently gathering us into his master plan, embraces the way of incongruity, dwelling amongst our disarray, our disaffections and our denials of all that is holy and true. Too often, popular devotion, including the greatest hymnody,[21] fails to register the pattern and instead of disclosing the brush marks of a sublime artist offers an image of the creation as one of serene and effortless activity – the fixed and final works of an almighty hand providing a purpose for everything without too much cost to the creator. The image fails to convince because it has no conception of the refractory things in the world that always elude the neat categories of the useful, decent and beautiful, and it conveys no sense whatsoever of the immense effort that is entailed in any creative work. At the human level we know that crafting a decent sonnet, shaping a passable poem, composing a piece of music that will move the hearer, even writing this solitary page, can be an exacting process. Once we begin to conjecture, however, what might be involved in making and sustaining a world of unimaginable scale in which order, oddness and playfulness are held together in such a way that outcomes cannot be guaranteed, are we not obliged to interpret it as the greatest labour of love? To see the creation as a costly work is to reject its presumed conformity to some predetermined plan discharged with casual care. It is also to take issue with the earlier objection of Peter Atkins: a lazy God could not have contemplated the stupendous effort of bringing into being that which was not there before. And an altogether careless deity can hardly be reconciled with the generosity of a God who 'animates eternal years . . . changes, sustains, dissolves, creates and rears'.[22] The words belong to Emily Brontë; in fact they are the last lines she ever wrote. The whole poem, 'Last Lines', is charged with awe and gratitude occasioned by her knowledge of the wastes and wonders of the world and the deep truth within her – the 'God within my breast' – that, even if everything ceased to be, still 'every existence would exist in thee'.[23] Every existence, all created things, everything that has breath, is now and for ever incorporated into the being of a universe formed by boundless energy and precarious endeavour. It seems to me that faith gains more than it loses when this way of looking at the world is embraced as the form of abundant living identified in the teaching of Jesus (Jn. 10.10). The stuff of life is *abundant* – there is just so much of it lurking beneath our feet, under stones and oceans and over our heads – utterly bewildering and fascinating in itself, but also pointing us to the many-splendoured thing, the great Sun we so often fail to see.

I have struggled with this opening chapter but the concluding lines have been written for me. Whether by chance or pleasing coincidence, they form part of the Collect for the Sunday facing me, the Second before Lent, and they will inform my sermon preparation:

> Almighty God, you have created the heavens and the earth and made us in your own image; teach us to discern your hand in all your works and your likeness in all your children.

When we read this prayer with Augustine and Annie Dillard in mind, the words suddenly come alive. And so do we.

2

Flexible Friends: Faith, Philosophy and the Life of the Mind

I hadn't expected Bertrand Russell to figure more than once in this book. After finishing the first chapter, however, I decided to delve into the Prologue of his autobiography again. It was easy to find on the internet and reading the words once more after so many years I can see why my youthful self was so animated by a text that seemed to be written in blood. It is too long to reproduce here in full but it still reads like an article of faith or a personal creed. For all Russell's avowed atheism, and the moral lapses of his private life, the Prologue bears a strong resemblance to a Christian vision of things. He begins by saying what he lived for: three passions governed his life – the longing for love; the search for knowledge; and an unbearable pity for the wretched of the earth, lives blighted by famine, torture and pain that made 'a mockery of what life should be'.[1] He realized that love could stave off the loneliness that pervades our human situation and even provide intimations of the heaven imagined by saints and poets. He longed to understand the mysteries of the human heart, why the stars shone in the sky and how it was, in his view, that the world of numbers and mathematics was more real than the universe itself. To prove the latter he spent 10 years writing *Principia Mathematica,* working between 7 and 10 hours a day, 6 days a week, often wondering if the task would ever be completed and occasionally prone to near suicidal despair.[2] The text ran to 4,500 pages and on completion had to be carried to the printers on a four-wheeled cart.[3] Books continued to flow from Russell's pen throughout his life. When he died in 1970 aged 97, more than 60 were still in print. In old age he also remained politically active, campaigning against war and nuclear weapons and the social evils that had caused him so much distress throughout his long and eventful life.

Whatever reservations we may have about Russell as a human being, he remains an interesting figure because he reminds us that part of our being properly human is bound up with the quest for understanding. By this I mean the attempt to make sense of reality, how we come to distinguish truth from falsehood or illusion and what it might mean to live a morally good life. These are uniquely human questions and it is difficult, if not impossible, to be human without engaging with them as we grow to maturity.

Russell's autobiography led me to his *History of Western Philosophy,*[4] a hugely ambitious work, highly opinionated, sometimes less than fair in its judgements but always informative. It instilled in me a desire to explore further. My pocket paperbacks began to multiply. Lunch breaks and train journeys introduced me to Socrates, Aristotle and Plato. Reading became a passion and I can still recall the excitement of engaging with outstanding minds that were very different in outlook but united by a concern to think about mortal questions, the questions which matter most.

Reading Marx and Nietzsche, Sartre and Camus, Kierkegaard and Wittgenstein opened a new world and also placed a considerable strain on a growing romance. I became so engrossed in a text when travelling that occasionally I would fail to get off at the train station where my future wife would be patiently waiting for a boyfriend who was much further down the line than he realized! Years later I took degrees in philosophy and philosophical theology and had the bracing experience of studying a number of influential thinkers in depth. Some have remained friends, mentors and interlocutors and not all of them have been kindly disposed to the claims of religion. Quite apart from their ideas I also became interested in their personalities and temperaments.[5] It was revealing to see how the intellectual outlook of a great thinker sometimes owes much to upbringing and early years. The philosophy of Arthur Schopenhauer is famously pessimistic[6] but this should not surprise us when we learn from his mother Joanne that, from an early age, her son 'brooded on the misery of things'.[7] Ludwig Wittgenstein is now regarded as the twentieth century's most important western philosopher despite the fact that he professed little formal knowledge of the classic philosophical texts. But he is remembered and revered as a dramatic and intense teacher who was not afraid of being wrong and who, on more than one occasion, gave up philosophy for school teaching and gardening in an Austrian monastery.[8]

Since 1990 I have been teaching philosophy to a wide range of students in a variety of settings under the broad heading of faith and understanding. The aim in every case has been to explore how Christian faith and the life of the mind connect or, to put it another way, how theology and philosophy can take

17

us on the inner and outer journey that represent the exciting and challenging call to discipleship. The contribution of students is always vital to the process: philosophy, as I have come to understand it and try to teach it, is neither some dry, academic subject nor an exercise in careful systematic thinking leading to tidy conclusions. It is instead an approach to life that sees questions as part of the human search for wisdom and meaning. The word *philia* in philosophy means a lover, someone passionately concerned to make sense of things in the knowledge that this entails endless reflection and the humbling admission of how little we actually know. Students bring their concerns and through lectures, conferences and seminars we engage in a continuing conversation which addresses the issues and questions that do not go away, that often impose themselves on us uninvited and sometimes keep us awake beyond the midnight hour. In a post-9/11 world, I have been particularly keen to explore issues of truth and trust, and how ideas have the power to reshape the world. In an article to mark the fifth anniversary of the terrorist attack on the Twin Towers, *The Economist* reminded its readers that it took just 19 men possessed of a consuming idea – *jihad* – to storm the economic citadels of America and usher in a very modern reign of terror. Ideas can be life giving or death dealing, able to promote good or evil alike in a way that far exceeds the power of vested interests. No less importantly, they help us to map the boundaries of a world that is stranger and crazier than we think through their insistence that, ultimately, life is either meaningful, tragic or absurd. In this respect the philosopher Friedrich Nietzsche opted for pessimism, as we can see from a passage formulated in his youth:

Once upon a time on a little star in a distant corner of the universe, clever little animals invented for themselves proud words like truth and goodness. But soon enough, the little star cooled, and the little animals had to die and with them their proud words. But the universe, never missing a step, drew another breath and moved on, dancing its cosmic dance across endless skies.[9]

I used this story quite recently to introduce Nietzsche to an enthusiastic evening class of mature students. It raises the questions of whether anyone knows we are here or care; whether faith can be sustained if such a haunting possibility exists; whether, paradoxically, this gently mocking evocation of apparent cosmic indifference actually helps to bolster faith as faith which only ever sees in part?[10] The evening went well and it succeeded in demonstrating how the cluster of questions bind theology and philosophy together. Both have things to say about the Nietzschean parable; both are passionately interested in the questions of God and how we might be human now; both for the greater part of their intellectual history have regarded the search for truth, meaning and beauty as an irresistible human imperative. Their common agenda arises out of a world inviting some sort of explanation and a sense of wonder that there is a world at all, instead of endless nothingness. And so the questions come rushing to meet us: does a creation presuppose a Creator? What keeps it going? And why, if, as Nietzsche insists, there is no benign impulse behind the world, do we feel so acutely our awareness of moral obligation – the still small voice of conscience that urges us to rise above self-interest and do the right thing? How strange it is that such habits of the heart endure if there is nothing above us except a dark cloud of futility. Even Nietzsche responded to the plight of a horse being beaten by a cab driver in the Piazza Carlo Alberto in Turin in January 1889. He flung himself around the horse's neck – a possible expression of creaturely feeling? – before collapsing to the ground. The man who had staked his reputation on the belief that life is about the will to power – a kind of cruel tendency towards self-assertion whatever the human consequences – was not beyond the claims of compassion or, morally speaking, the idea that to stand and watch a helpless creature being injured by its cruel owner was just plain wrong.

The decision on my part to use conversation and questions as a process whereby faith secures a greater depth and coherence that reflect and respect our God-given capacity for rational thought has a long pedigree. In Chapter 1 I referred to Augustine's propensity to 'think in questions'. My own mind has also been shaped by the approach of Thomas Aquinas, now regarded by the Roman Catholic Church as its greatest thinker.[11] He lived a short life during a time of great intellectual ferment in the thirteenth century yet still managed to produce a remarkable body of work running to millions of words. His output constituted a rediscovery and reformulation of the works of Aristotle that had become available in the West again after centuries of neglect. His mind was so fertile that his dictation could occupy up to four secretaries – one tradition even recorded that he composed in his sleep. His intellectual formation as a Dominican friar had convinced him that in order for faith to be taken seriously by non-Christians it had to appeal not only to revelation but reason. In writing as he did, and it is shown most prominently in his unfinished masterwork *Summa theologiae* (Summation of Theology),[12] his purpose was practical and down to earth. He did not have sophisticated university audiences in mind but Dominican novices and the matters that concerned ordinary people in their strengths and weaknesses. His approach is a convincing example of the creative interplay of theology and philosophy in the life of faith. Although he believed that the latter rested upon a revealed truth disclosed in Scripture and the teaching of the Church, he also recognized his responsibility as a Christian thinker to respond to intellectual and moral difficulties which could be answered. Two features of his method are particularly interesting and relevant to the aim of this chapter. First, like Augustine before him, Aquinas moves from one question to another with an infectious eagerness. He is always asking 'Why?' or 'What?' and a case can be made for viewing his whole system of thinking as resting on a question. The central element in his work is God, but he is not satisfied simply to confess that God is and 'chooses instead to explore the divine in as many ways as possible'.[13] Secondly, his output embraces problems that still reflect many of our basic concerns: God, the nature of truth, existence, other people, and our common destiny as fellow-travellers who frequently lose our bearings in the dark wood that is the world. To this end he never flinches from the difficult questions posed by those who do not share his faith or his presuppositions. The image of him that I cherish most is that of the Dominican scholar at his desk with the manuscript of his great *Summa* open to view. His writing displays its usual clarity and, as he sets down his propositions that are intended to provide the faithful with good reasons for what they profess to believe, he momentarily stops before introducing into the wide, clean margin of his manuscript the two best arguments he can find against his position. He goes back to the manuscript and answers the objections. In this way he is constantly striving to be truthful: there is truth to be handed on but there are also questions to be answered if faith in God and the business of being human are to be faced with real integrity.

Encouraged by Aquinas I must now be daring enough to deal with the possible objections to my own approach to doing theology and forming faith from a philosophical perspective. I can think of three, two of which are, unsurprisingly, interconnected. The first dates back to Tertullian, a great theologian of the second century[14] who famously and dismissively posed the question 'What is there in common between Athens and Jerusalem?'[15] For him Christianity was essentially bound up with the revelation of God in Christ and therefore had no need of the wisdom or philosophy of the Greeks, however estimable or profound their thought. To put it rather crudely: if our faith rests on a revelation, who needs reason? There are two answers to this objection: firstly, faith as a supernatural gift from God is always required to understand what it believes in order to save it from laziness, blindness, stupidity or (and this is very apposite in a post-9/11 world) the worst excesses of religious fanaticism that lead to cruel intolerance and innocent deaths. Secondly, philosophical reason is the proper and natural means that God has given us to clarify, refine and where necessary purge our understanding in order that faith does not fall prey to believing 'six impossible things before breakfast'.[16] Aquinas grasps this very well. Without relinquishing his belief in a supernatural agency – miracles, providence, Scripture, God's presence in things – he is also resolute that we should always begin by paying close attention to what is actually evident to our senses in the world around us and reason from such data to God. He concedes that reason cannot take us all the way – philosophy does have its limitations – but it is at that point that theology (aided by divine grace) takes its hand and completes its endeavours. By then reason has done its job, pointing us to the invisible things of God from the visible phenomena of the world.[17] A parallel can be drawn here with Augustine who is quick to point his readers to all that is good in pagan philosophy. Although some of its tenets have no immediate relevance to Christianity, we are nevertheless obliged to acknowledge truth wherever we find it:

> Pagan learning is not entirely made up of false teachings and superstitions . . . It contains also some excellent teachings, well suited to be used by truth, and excellent moral values. Indeed, some truths are even found among them which relate to the worship of the one God. Now these are, so to speak, their gold and their silver, which they did not invent themselves, but which they dug out of the mines of the providence of God, which are scattered throughout the world, yet which are improperly and unlawfully prostituted to the worship of demons. The Christian, therefore, can separate these truths from their unfortunate associations, take them away, and put them to their proper use for the proclamation of the gospel . . . [18]

Any lingering doubts on the part of the reader concerning the legitimacy of this approach – that we should expect and seek illumination outside the ark of the Church – are dealt with by Augustine through a scriptural reference to Moses. As a most faithful servant of God he had done the same thing and it was written of him that 'he was learned in all the wisdom of the Egyptians' (Acts 7.22).

Scripture brings us appropriately to the second objection: why study philosophy when we have a Bible that contains all that is necessary for our edification and guides us unerringly to the person of Jesus as 'the way, and the truth, and the life'? (Jn. 14.6). Without trading too much, I hope, on their name and reputation, it does seem to me that Augustine and Aquinas have already answered this question. There is the Book of God – or, to be more theologically nuanced – a Book about God containing a diverse range of texts drawn from different times and sources. This we seek to honour, for it retains its ancient power and spiritual authority to direct us 'to the infinite God whose understanding no human being can fathom and who stands in judgement on all our claims that somehow we have captured ultimate truth'.[19] But, as theologians from the earliest centuries have reminded us, there is also the Book of Nature that evokes in us a fascination with things and draws us beyond itself to the sovereign Lord of all that is. And, arguably, closest of all to us, there is the Book of Life – the unending cycle of innocence and experience, joy and sorrow, hope and despair through which we come to recognize not only our moral frailty as persons but also our longings which find their home in the realm of the eternal. Revelation comes in subtle guises, at times wearing the cloak of Scripture or manifesting itself in a grain of sand; or yet again in the unexpected peace that passes all understanding, even when all human hope has gone.

The third and final objection comes in the form of a contemporary challenge that questions the limits of philosophy and that of language itself in relation to what we might call truth-seeking. In the role of devil's advocate we are confronted by the eminent American philosopher Richard Rorty, who for several decades has been preoccupied by how language works and what we can reasonably expect from it as a tool for understanding the way the world is.[20] Rorty is a pragmatist: he believes that language cannot claim definitively or even accurately to represent reality as some sort of 'mirror of nature'. All claims to truth and knowledge of reality are in his view tentative and provisional and there is no way of getting beyond language in order to see the world as it 'really' is. Whatever we mean by 'the world' it is always more mysterious, elusive and complex than we realize and it is a conceit on our part to suppose that it can be contained within the net of language. What language does is to help us *cope* with reality rather than *copy* it. When we engage in philosophy it is a mistake on our part to suppose that we are going to discover what is out there or, indeed, any common realization of the truth of how we ought to live.

Let me first admit that I am rather taken with the clever and insightful distinction that Rorty draws between *coping* and *copying*. Words do help us to cope when our experience is messy and our way unclear. I shall have more to say about this in a later chapter. I also need to say, however, that I have no intention, now or in the foreseeable future, of relegating my philosophy classes to the status of a reading group enjoying civilized conversation without any pretence that steps have been made or can be made towards making sense of the world or the human condition. I have no plans in this direction for three good reasons. First, with some notable exceptions – justice and beauty, for example – I have never believed that the task of philosophy is to arrive at hard definitions. We do need to know what justice is if we are to act justly and we need to be able to recognize beauty if we are to reject what is aesthetically counterfeit or second-rate. Philosophy can help and guide us here. With regard to issues of a spiritual world, however, a guiding hand behind the appearance of things, an entity we call the soul that makes us more than conspicuous limbs and organs, the sheer unexplained existence of matter and the brute reality of evil, philosophy, like theology, should proceed with tact and deference, always conscious of the limitations of language in relation to life's *ultimates*, and acutely aware that every philosophical conversation concludes with questions we still find puzzling. Augustine knew that human words always fall short in relation to the mystery of God and that whatever can be said about reality is only ever an approximation. But he also recognized the paradox contained in the human need to speak of things we do not fully understand, even in the knowledge that we can never grasp that which our words are directed towards and seek to describe.

In consequence there is no suggestion that my philosophy meetings are holding up a mirror to nature to reflect its countenance in every detail. We have been trying to map the world in the knowledge that our map will frequently bear scant resemblance to what actually exists. Philosophy is an exercise in humility rather than hubris and this fact alone vitiates a good deal of Rorty's criticism.

Being humble does not entail that we are entirely ignorant as we wrestle with imponderables. My second response to Rorty has to do with the further fact that philosophical conversation enriches the life of the mind. It introduces us to other minds that are also committed to truth-seeking. We are admitted to other worlds, other ways of seeing and experiencing that constitute not only an enlargement of our sensibilities but also our understanding. The pursuit of truth is a communal exercise made all the richer by the insights and illuminations that are not of our own devising. Without contradiction we can speak of a deeper awareness that in a modest way has the force of a revelation: the 'penny drops' so to speak, there is an 'Ah' moment and we see more clearly. We are, after all, engaging (historically speaking) with great minds that have devoted their not inconsiderable genius to concerns that have lost none of their relevance for those attracted to the path of wisdom. My feelings about the value of philosophy are reflected in the following words of the writer Jane Smiley, as she describes the reward of reading a demanding text:

> When I have read a long novel, when I have entered systematically into a sensibility which is alien to mine, the author's or a character's, when I have become interested in a person because he is interesting . . . there is a possibility that at the end I will be a degree less self-centred . . . a degree more able to see the world as another sees it. And there is a possibility that I will be able to reason about my own emotions. In

the end I will be more empathetic . . . more sympathetic.[21]

Words retain a power to reconfigure our world by enabling us to view things from another perspective. Philosophy in this respect does more than help us cope with reality. It can bring us to a closer approximation of the nature of things by reminding us that our apparent inability to make sense of the world will sometimes reflect the fact that we are simply asking the wrong questions. This is an important contribution and effectively constitutes my third rejoinder to Rorty. When serious misfortune assails us, a common reaction is to say, 'Why has this happened to me?' Bewilderment and often self-pity go hand in hand with outrage and indignation. The unwarranted presumption made in such situations is that creator and creation alike are judged in terms of how adequately they provide for our well-being and security. Philosophy tries tactfully to point out that we are not bound to view the world this way. We are each but a small entity in a vast interconnected whole and as such we are subject to its laws, to microbes and viruses and, finally, to death. Much of this is beyond our control and our real freedom consists in the type of response we make to perceived misfortune. We may still choose to shake our fist at fate but philosophy teaches us there is also another way.

The intractable nature of the world and the choices we make in response to its perceived unfairness serve to demonstrate another feature of philosophy: it is, or should be, practical in its application, of real service to us as we negotiate the pitfalls that attend our lives, and a source of wisdom that enables us to live without fear, resentment or illusions. Philosophy, like faith, must be practised and performed, which is another way of saying that its utility is best demonstrated in the crucible of daily living.

Last evening I called on a family grief-stricken by the loss of their 20-year-old son who had taken his own life just three weeks earlier. I noticed on sitting down that the calendar on the wall had not been changed for four days – a visible reminder to a caller like myself that in this house time had been frozen and the days had lost their meaning. The family and close neighbours had required a lot of care following this tragic and senseless death. We took time over the organization of his service and dealt as best we could with all the hard questions, including his destiny beyond the grave. The funeral took place in church on a rainy, windswept day with hundreds of his young friends in attendance. It was a stark but dignified occasion and in my address I urged the youthful congregation to view life as a gift and to live in such a way that their days should be full and long. And with regard to the friend they were remembering, I reminded them of the story of the Prodigal Son and the love of his father who bore no thoughts of condemnation towards his wayward child.

The following evening a concert was held in church featuring an accomplished jazz trio on a national tour of cathedrals and other places of worship. As I sat in the audience enjoying the ethereal sound and the subdued lighting it struck me quite powerfully that the players were performing in exactly the same space that some 24 hours earlier had been occupied by a young man's coffin. What could I make of this? In the internal conversation that followed a number of scenarios emerged. The jazz trio constituted clear evidence of the irrepressible surge of life, the disquieting but inescapable fact that life goes on, undistracted by our personal griefs and sorrows, forever busying itself with new experiences that constitute the present moment, and seemingly indifferent to the tragedy that had brought such a large gathering to this place the previous day. Nietzsche's parable about the little star in a distant corner of the universe where proud words and fragile lives peter out and die as the universe moves on 'without missing a step' seemed to reflect the pathos of the scene. Words from Psalm 103, a text that is frequently used at funerals, also came to mind: 'As for man, his days are as grass: as a flower of the field, so he flourisheth. For the wind passeth over it, and it is gone; and the place thereof shall know it no more' (Ps. 103.15–16, KJV). The haunting vision of a philosopher who had come to believe that God was dead, combined with the unflinching realism of the psalmist well acquainted with the transience and decay that constitute our common destiny as persons, provided a sombre reminder of the brevity of life and the marked disinclination of the world to remember anyone for very long.

I continued thinking: this young man in his untimely death had nothing to fear from this scenario. Even if Nietzsche was right – if all existence is nothing more than an inexorable movement towards death in a world that cares not at all about our dreams or destinies – there is nevertheless a strange comfort to be had from the realization that the universe is neither for us nor against us. The stars just shine down: our happiness, misfortune or demise are none of their concern. They have other business in their 'endless skies' and this fact alone is consoling for anyone, young or old, who thinks the world is intent on cutting them down or who has ever feared that their misdeeds will be held against them by the unforgiving force of fate or destiny. Philosophy had cleared the ground a little for me as I ruminated while the trio played on beautifully. And then in a final scene – and here I go back to Aquinas – reason, having accomplished its work, gave way to theology to 'complete its endeavours'. The supplementary verse of the psalm that I quoted earlier came back to me. Having acknowledged that we are but passing shadows with no natural claim to immortality it continues: 'But the merciful goodness of the Lord endures for ever and ever and his righteousness is upon their children's children' (Ps. 103.17). The divine mercy extends over all things – the unfeeling stars and the tragic lapses of youth. God is, and in his goodness remains, for us (Rom. 8.31).

3

Some Hidden Prophetic Intention: Providence and Purpose

I need to begin with a word of explanation about the title of this chapter. For me it evokes a period of my life that at the time and in retrospect represented a time of wonder. To be alive then was 'very heaven'. Poetry and philosophy had staked their claims on my life, I had travelled across America and after a broken romance was moving in new circles. I had always been passionately fond of popular music and remain thankful that I lived through the heady days of Beatlemania. A new friendship, however, with someone more knowledgeable than myself introduced me to classical music. I had already come to appreciate the works of Elgar and Handel but thanks to Peter I was initiated into the symphonies of Mahler, Brahms, Shostakovitch and Nielsen, the operas of Wagner and the chamber works of Janáček. My enthusiasm grew and I began to make further discoveries of my own. The music of Ralph Vaughan Williams took hold of me and I can still recall the shock I felt on listening for the first time to the opening bars of his *Sea Symphony*. The music is set to the poetry of Walt Whitman.[1] His evocation of the sea and those who sail upon its restless waters serves as a metaphor for the journey of the human soul as it navigates the uncharted and mysterious deeps that bring it ultimately to the safe harbour of a transcendent God. I have remembered a fair amount of the poetry and it has found its way into my sermons and lectures. In Part 4 of the symphony, a baritone and soprano represent explorers contemplating the power and beauty of sea and sky. Above them is the unending procession of sun and moon and countless stars and below the teeming grass and waters. Their thoughts begin to turn to God, for this beautiful vista seems to disclose 'some hidden prophetic intention'. The symphony closes with the music dissolving into silence and we are left with the vision of the soul bound where no mariner has gone. Concert audiences are never quite sure when to clap but the one thing they know as the notes fade is the conviction of Whitman that our little lives and deaths are set within a providential order. God's purposes may often be hidden or unclear but behind the appearance of things it is still possible to glimpse a veiled but benign intention. We can risk everything as we set forth, for all seas are the seas of God.

My concern in what follows is to test this assertion – to explore, in other words, how faith is grounded in the belief that God acts purposefully, that his fingerprints can be seen on the amazing, brittle and crazy events that make up our lives; that we can without blatant contradiction speak of divine providence. There are days, of course, when none of this presents a problem and our waking hours bring intimations of Eden. We know ourselves to be blessed: we ask and it is given to us; we knock and the door is opened; we seek and we find (Matt. 7.7–9). The gospel promises ring true. But we must also contend with days of suffering, moments when the creation seems deformed by evil and periods of melancholy or sheer uneventfulness.[2] To have faith that there is 'some hidden prophetic intention' is to open ourselves to risk and a level of honesty that is not to be confused with frankness or sincerity. Faith demands what Andrew Shanks has described in his recent book as *radical* honesty – an openness to how the world really is and 'what other people may have to say'.[3] The precariousness of an ostensibly good earth frequently calls divine providence into question. At 9.15 a.m. on Friday 21 October 1966 a monstrous waste tip coursed down a mountain into the mining community of Aberfan. A school stood in its way. The children were returning from assembly when the tide overwhelmed them. One hundred and sixteen pupils died along with five teachers. In assembly they had been singing 'All things bright and beautiful'. I wrote a poem at the time that expressed my own bewilderment and sadness and I can still see the news picture of a distraught police officer bearing in his arms the lifeless body of a child. During my ministry I have tried to listen honestly to the voices of protest with their insistence that such tragedies call into question the goodness and omnipotence of God. The problem of evil and the calamity of chance events do not sit well with our moral sensibilities or the nagging conviction that a loving father of unsurpassed power should organize things better. Religion has often countenanced patience in the face of suffering and the importance of a heavenly perspective as we pass through this vale of earthly misery (Ps. 84.6). In Schiller's poem 'Ode to Joy' we read:

> Be patient, O millions!
> Be patient for the better world!

34

> There above the starry sky
> A great God will give a reward.[4]

Quite probably millions of souls have been prepared to follow this spiritual injunction in the belief that the sorrows that diminished them in life would find both resolution and reward in the hereafter. In more recent times, however, we have witnessed the emergence of a particular kind of objection to the notion of heavenly compensation that goes under the name of *protest atheism*. Its classical expression can be found in the story told by Ivan Karamazov in Dostoevsky's novel *The Brothers Karamazov*. Ivan tells of a poor serf child who hits his master's dog with a stone as he is playing. The master has the boy seized and the next morning he is torn to pieces before his mother's eyes. Ivan is not consoled by the argument that heaven will somehow make amends for the child's suffering. The admission ticket to the celestial city cannot be accepted if there is no righteousness in the world. In his view, there is no harmony – on earth or in heaven – that could ever justify the death of even one child, and so Ivan respectfully returns the ticket:

> We cannot afford to pay so much for admission . . . And indeed if I am an honest man, I'm bound to hand it back as soon as possible . . . I accept God, understand that, but I cannot accept the world he has made.[5]

Ivan is radically honest, constrained on the one hand by an innate sense of justice which finds the torture and death of a child morally unacceptable and, on the other, convinced that Christian grammar must from now on forego such expressions as divine benevolence or divine providence. Is he right? Before we rush to our religious barricades in order to defend one of our most cherished assumptions – that the world is held within God's all pervasive and sustaining presence – faith is required to stop and think. It really does matter for the sake of truth and honesty that we know what we are talking about when the discussion engages with the tragic dimension of life and the extent to which it denies that the world is the work of a morally good God. Two preliminary considerations are in order before we try to make headway.

Firstly, we should note the distinction customarily made in the treatment of moral evil and that of natural evil or suffering. The former may be seen as human wickedness in all its forms – torture (Ivan again), terrorism and genocide spring immediately to mind. Moral evil is what we originate through our thoughts and actions. The latter, on the other hand, cannot easily be ascribed to human agency. Monsoons and plagues, cancers and catastrophes of every kind, from a tsunami wave to Hurricane Katrina, are part of the natural order and constitute a threat to all forms of life. There is a further category: that of complex evil. Suffering sometimes occurs through human wilfulness and indifference but on other occasions it may be a consequence of inertia. Hurricane Katrina brought awful devastation in its path but damage could have been minimized if government funding had been made available earlier to erect flood barriers that were demonstrably necessary but financially prohibitive. The boundary between moral and natural evil is neither simple nor clear-cut and human motives are frequently ambiguous.[6]

Secondly, we need to dispose of the impostors that frequently masquerade as providence. I am thinking here of how providence has come to be confused or conflated with terms that on the surface appear identical or similar but, theologically speaking, are very different. So we are disposing of lady luck, fortune's wheel, the roll of the dice, a wistful resignation to fate or destiny and, most emphatically, (from a religious viewpoint), the cruel doctrine of predestination. This last category has always perturbed me not least because of its terrible hold on the Christian imagination down the centuries. A couple of evenings ago I gave a lecture on the philosopher Søren Kierkegaard. We began by exploring the grim melancholy that had shaped his formative years. This was largely due to his old and neurotic father who, as a boy of 12 minding the sheep, had climbed up a hill and cursed God. This act of rebellion cast a long and dismal shadow over his life. Despite the material success he later enjoyed as a public figure of some repute, he was inwardly shattered by guilt and remorse, convinced that his rebellion against God had initiated an inexorable chain of tragic events. He attributed the death of his first wife and the successive deaths of his children to an almost mechanistic conception of divine providence. Imprisoned by a narrow predestinarian theology he interpreted the loss of his loved ones in terms of a punishment for the blasphemy of his early youth. Søren was not a melancholy child but there is no doubt that the brooding atmosphere of his home life, in large part generated by his father, influenced his thinking to the end of his short life.

We have cleared the ground a little. By eliminating impostors and thinking more carefully about the complex relationship between moral and natural evil we are now better placed to say what belief in providence amounts to. I want to avoid too sharp a definition but as I reflect again on that marvellous canvas evoked by the poetry of Whitman and the music of Vaughan Williams, it lures me in the direction of a God who cares for all his creation, providing for its needs and guiding its destiny, including our lives within it. If a sense of providential order lies at the heart of the religious life, it is because we grasp with Whitman that 'all seas are the seas of God'. To put this in biblical terms, God continues to act towards God's creation with the same intent and in the same spirit that brought things into being. The world is a conspicuous labour of love on God's part: 'all things were made by him; and without him was not any thing made that was made' (Jn. 1.3, KJV). Providence is therefore an extension of the doctrine of creation and it reflects the religious conviction that God does not cease from God's labours or relinquish the object of God's love. These truths constitute the source of our gratitude for the many gifts we receive in life and also inform our prayer. We are not to be over-anxious because the creation declares that God cares for the smallest of things:

> I tell you, do not worry about your life, what you will eat or what you will drink, or about your body, what you will wear. Look at the birds of the air; they neither sow nor reap nor gather into barns, and yet your heavenly Father feeds them. Are you not of more value than they? (Matt. 6.25–26)

These words tell us something about the Jewishness of Jesus; about his adherence to the worship of the synagogue that celebrated the changing seasons and the dependability of God; and, no less, the knowledge of his own scriptures with their prolific images of God's benign oversight of the world. The psalmist is frequently moved to praise:

You make springs gush forth in the valleys,
they flow between the hills,
giving drink to every wild animal;
the wild asses quench their thirst . . .
You cause the grass to grow for the cattle,
    and plants
for people to use,
to bring forth food from the earth,
and wine to gladden the human heart.

                        (Ps. 104.10–11, 14–15)

God cares, but the scriptures also go on to affirm that God guides and summons. Abraham has to leave his own country for a far land that the Lord will show him (Genesis 12.1). Moses is despatched (against his wishes) to Pharaoh to bring about the liberation of the Israelites (Ex. 4.10–13). God calls Israel out of Egypt and promises them a land flowing with milk and honey (Ex. 3.8). The apostle Paul has a night vision that stops him in his tracks: a man beseeches him to 'Come over to Macedonia and help us' (Acts 16.9). Paul ditches his plan to travel to Bithynia and immediately heads for Macedonia 'being convinced that God had called us to proclaim the good news to them' (Acts 16.10).

The summons, or call, lies at the heart of Christian vocation. We sometimes feel compelled by a force that is not of ourselves, whose nature is unquestionably good. Demands are made upon us that, left unacknowledged, refuse to give us peace of mind. We may be unclear concerning the outcome of our response but what we cannot doubt is the veracity of the demand. I keep the following prayer from the Lutheran tradition in my Bible:

Lord God,
you have called your servants
to ventures of which we cannot see the ending
by paths as yet untrodden.
Give us faith to go out with good courage,
not knowing where we go
but only that your hand is leading us
and your love supporting us;
through Jesus Christ our Lord. Amen.[7]

Barely past my mid-twenties I knew that my useful and satisfying career in personnel management was no longer to be my life's work. Despite my intellect and instincts recoiling against the idea of ordination I offered myself for ministerial training. Initial enquiries on my part and subsequent interviews proved unsatisfactory and I left the idea alone. The promptings continued. Eventually I gave in and after a relatively short period found myself at theological college. Throughout this period of questioning and testing there were no dramatic experiences or visions, just a growing sense of something very deep within me that seemed to be pointing to a new direction for my life. About 10 years later, when I was immersed in the demands of my second parish, all this came back to me as I read a moving account of how another Anglican priest experienced a providential hand upon his shoulder:

> . . . as the weeks and months went by and I heard appeals from the pulpit Sunday by Sunday for people to volunteer for the ministry, I found it progressively difficult to see any good reason why I should not at least offer myself; but since I could also see no good reason why I should do so, I remained

in a state of indecision. Then, one day in the early 1950s after I had spent some time in silence in the London house of a monastic order of Anglican monks, I went to see my mother, who was recovering from a minor operation in a nursing home. I travelled on the top of a bus, and as it made its way up the Tottenham Court Road I was overcome by the same sort of experience that I had had years ago in the suburban train near Bromley; once again, the dingy landscape became transparent to something other than itself, and as I looked at the small forest of dreary Victorian church spires pointing upwards to the grey London sky over the desert of urban roof-tops which stretched away to the wrecked horizon, I knew that I had to identify myself with them. They were symbols of hope in a dry land: hope whether the people of London, for whom they pointed their stony fingers to God, knew it or not: hope that the ordinary men and women who lived there, like the London spires, were also pointers to God for those with eyes to see the hidden truth of them. When I told my wife that I had decided to offer myself for ordination, she sat down and asked me for a drink.[8]

I have no recollection now as to whether my wife made the same request but I recognized in the passage my own identification with the urban landscape, the possibilities of grace and hope within its dingy streets and the desire to serve and make a difference. This brings home to me the crucial link between our belief in providence and human action. For most of us, most of the time, the guiding hand that desires our human flourishing has to be discerned within the web of human relationships that make up our lives, the particular interpretations we give to our experiences –'Was that really just chance or something more?' – the showing of love towards our neighbour and the life of prayer that make us co-workers with God (2 Cor. 6.1) and participants in divine activity.

None of this is to suggest that an age of miracles is past and therefore to be consigned to the pages of Scripture along with the burning bush and the pillar of cloud or fire that led the people of Israel out of captivity (Ex. 13.21–22). Faith has to be open to the action of God that we can describe only in forms of *special providence,* the mysterious interventions that bring life and healing when all human hope and ingenuity have gone and remind us all over again of the central miracle of the resurrection of Jesus from the dead. But faith must also be brave enough to recognize that 'without us God will not; without us God cannot',[9] which is to say that, most frequently, the creative, revealing and redeeming acts of God emerge out of our partnership with God and the extent to which God's hands work through ours to bring about the good of others. St Paul expresses this in terms of a basic belief: 'We *know* that all things work together for good for those who love God, who are called according to his purpose' (Rom. 8.28). Like many pastors, I can testify to the occasions when I have been humbled into awe and silence as the personal suffering of others has become a means of spiritual and moral growth. It is hard to resist this conclusion. Individuals and sometimes whole communities can, and do, learn more of themselves and their potentialities in a time of pestilence. And for some, their pain is a means of identification with the innocent figure of Jesus who accepted everything 'even death on a cross' (Phil. 2.8) before he entered into glory. These facts have led some eminent theologians to place human ills within a providential scheme. Following Plato, both Augustine and Aquinas maintained that darkness is needed to appreciate the light, pain to remind us of the pleasure of vibrant health and suffering to make full use of times of well-being.

My pen falters a little at this point: I can see that suffering can be educative, that we can become stronger when darkness overtakes us. But I must also concede that this is not always the case. I know as a pastor that suffering sometimes diminishes individuals to the extent that, with Job, they have neither 'ease nor rest' and regret the day they were born (Job 3.3–26). If they welcome death it is not because they feel themselves to be safe in the arms of Jesus but rather that they need to be free from an existence that has become intolerable. Searching through some old research papers as background for this chapter, I came across the following extract from Somerset Maugham based on his experiences as he trained to be a doctor:

> I set down in my notebooks not once or twice, but in a dozen places the facts that I had seen. I know that suffering did not ennoble; it degraded. It made men selfish, mean, petty, and suspicious. It absorbed them in small things and made them less than men.[10]

It seems to me incongruous, if not actually immoral, to dignify such awful situations by suggesting that they are somehow part of God's good creation and therefore providential. Consequently, I have some sympathy for Ivan Karamazov and his radical honesty that will not allow him to entertain the contradiction in a religious point of view that in its defence of a good and all powerful God and the consolation of heaven is prepared along the way to justify or defend all sorts of moral enormities. We are back to the questions that Ivan's honesty provokes: how can we tolerate even the death of one innocent child and somehow still go on to speak of a providential framework surrounding our lives and ultimate destinies? Would it not simply be better to accept the churning chaos and unfairness of the world and leave out any references to 'some hidden prophetic intention' that faith has traditionally associated with God?

Because Ivan speaks for many sensitive souls on these issues, his questions cannot be lightly cast aside. In reply I would wish to say that in the first instance, the suffering or death of any child can never be regarded as acceptable, necessary or instrumental in relation to God's will for his world. Such a view would cast God in the role of tyrant or despot and in no way to be identified with the outpouring of love that we identify with the ministry of Jesus who in proclaiming the kingdom, healed the sick, brought sight to the blind and raised the daughter of Jairus to life (Mk. 5.35–42). I speak here as a father who has held the dead body of his own daughter in his hands and also shared the prolonged sadness occasioned by repeated miscarriages. In none of these instances did it make any sense for my wife and I to interpret them as manifestations of God's purposes towards us. They represented nature gone awry; we had to endure, hope and learn.

Secondly, the chaos and unfairness of the world, real as they are, need to be set alongside the more fundamental truth that a good deal of the time we find ourselves in a 'relatively stable and ordered environment in which we have come to feel, so to speak, at home'.[11] If we presume to know God by faith it is not because of some rare or private experience but rather through our awareness of *significance* – that fundamental aspect of our experience which enables us to trust the world because it is a familiar and intelligible place where we may hope to live and flourish in a right relationship with the rest of the created order. When bad things happen we often forget that our sadness and dismay also reflect the unacknowledged fact that tragedy is the exception not the norm: nature gone awry is not the way nature normally operates. Order, regularity, dependability: these are the endearing features of our external world and they constitute the bedrock of our experience – the night and day, the light and dark, the dependable earth and the constellations of the heavens that constitute God's theatre in which temporal ills have to be weighed against joys and blessings and personality may hope to reflect something of the divine life. When evils intrude and human potentialities are cut short, it is then that faith has to embrace a wider perspective. Only with the hope of heaven can we begin to hold on to a notion of providence which enables us to say that, although our present experiences may sometimes be utterly negative, they will ultimately be overcome. As Mother Julian of Norwich wrestled with the problem of evil, revelation came to her in these salutary words: 'Sin is necessary, but all shall be well, and all shall be well, and all manner of things shall be well.'[12]

It is important to understand the original context of these words. They might appear unduly optimistic, even glib, until we realize that Julian lived through three outbreaks of the Black Death, one of which halved the population of Norwich where she lived and prayed. She had no basis for believing that in the end God's designs would be fulfilled except for her conviction that the sorrows which hurt us now will find their ultimate resolution in the perspective of eternity. Unlike Ivan, she had no wish to return the admission ticket. Without the promise of a vista where there is neither sorrow nor crying, for the pain of former things has passed away, (Rev. 21.4) a belief in providence cannot ultimately be sustained. Heaven is the final vindication of God's love and it is only on the basis of this sublime vision of human redemption that we are finally entitled to speak of God's loving purposes in a world where injustices of various sorts lay waste many lives and children die.

I offer these responses to Ivan not in terms of irrefutable arguments to dismantle his positions but rather as suggestions that enable us to see his objections in a different light. It is not true that the only thing we are entitled to say about the creation is that it 'stands on absurdities . . . soaked from its crust to the centre with the tears of humanity'.[13] There are good and compelling reasons to celebrate the beauty and constancy of the world to the extent that if we are moved to speak about the 'tears of humanity' it is because they are sometimes occasioned by joy. Suffering is not the sole measure of reality, and the perplexing fact that evil has its counterparts of laughter, happiness, love and goodness as integral elements of human life can lead us naturally to an attitude of trust towards life itself and the trustworthy power underpinning all things.[14]

A power we should add – and this, crucially, seems to have escaped Ivan – that we do not confuse with the absolute power of the despot. Faith is predicated on a view of omnipotence that reveals itself in the paradox of the humility and suffering that attend the disclosure of God in Christ:

> In the end . . . we see the power, the wisdom, the presence of God in terms of his love and compassion: something that could never have been so seen apart from the incarnation.[15]

To believe in providence is to feel at home in the world and to trust in the God who reveals God's power in the weakness of the cross. It is to hope in that redemptive love which 'bears all things, believes all things . . . endures all things' and 'never ends' (1 Cor. 13.7,8) and it is to commit ourselves each new day to the work of prayer:

> Lord of life and love
> we live in the promise that
> you know our story better than we do.
> Often we see nothing in our story but
>   darkness
> and we long for your light.
> Hold on to us in the darkness,
> for the darkness is no darkness with you.
> Bring light to our story,
> the light of your healing providence,
> the light of the coming and creation of your
>   kingdom,
> the light which dawns in doing your will.
> Amen.[16]

4

Finding the Old Way Forward: History and Wisdom

April has ended gloriously. I am in America fulfilling speaking engagements, meeting with parish clergy and scholars and finishing writing assignments. Earlier this evening, with the sun still warm and an urgent breeze claiming the fragile blossom from the Manhattan trees, my wife and I walked on to the Brooklyn Bridge. I have been a frequent visitor to New York over the years but this was my first time over the bridge by foot. My younger son had made the same crossing a few weeks earlier and had insisted that we should follow in his footsteps. Somehow everything came magically together: the boats on the brilliant water, the majesty of the river and skyline, the flow of human traffic with the day's work ended and the spirit of place immortalized by the poets of an earlier century left us spellbound. Walt Whitman was mesmerized by this scene and it pleased him to think of those who would cross this water long after his death.[1]

The bridge remains an enduring testimony to daring human imagination and precision of thought. It grew out of the vision of a German immigrant and engineer, John Roebling, assisted by his son Washington, also an engineer and a survivor of the Civil War. Built by hand between 1869 and 1883, the construction employed 600 workers, 27 of whom died before its completion. When finished it represented the longest span in the world. It was praised from every quarter, but it is the following quotation from Thomas Kinsella of *The Brooklyn Eagle* in 1872 that has been set in stone close to where the crossing begins:

> When the perfected bridge shall permanently and uninterruptedly connect the two cities of New York and Brooklyn, the daily thousands who cross it will consider it a sort of natural and inevitable phenomena such as the rising and setting of the sun and they will consciously overlook the preliminary difficulties surmounted before the structure surmounted the stream and will perhaps undervalue the indomitable courage, the absolute faith, the consummate genius which assured the engineer's triumph.

I have no idea what religion Kinsella lived by but as I read his eulogy with my emotions still jangling from what I had seen and shared minutes earlier, the words seemed to resonate with the imagery and insights of Scripture. We are indebted to the past yet need to be reminded of it if the extraordinary is not to become commonplace through too casual an acquaintance. We so easily forget the cost that lies at the heart of any creative endeavour and fail to appreciate the remarkable human qualities that breathe life into a vision and give it legs to cross the generations. It is the journalist of a prominent Brooklyn newspaper speaking to us here. But I can also detect the distant voice of the prophets calling a careless people back to God, or St Paul pleading with his fledgling communities to live up to their calling, or the writer of Hebrews reminding pilgrims that their faith and confidence owe much to the arduous witness of those who have gone before. They are surrounded by a 'great cloud of witnesses' (Heb. 12.1) – those who trusted God and yielded up their lives in a time of darkness. As the pilgrims travel, they are also called to look back and remember the faith of the patriarchs, prophets and martyrs (Heb. 11). Their past represents a key to understanding their present identity and future hope as the people of God. Their history tells them who they are and what they might become.

For the last three weeks, as I have moved from pulpits to seminar rooms, talked to congregations and students and debated with distinguished individuals from different academic disciplines and religious traditions, the relationship between faith and history and the way in which the past continues to shape the present have never been far from my mind. These issues have fascinated me ever since I first read about Martin Luther and the impact of the sixteenth-century European Reformation more than 30 years ago. I recall very clearly walking from my college library early one autumnal Saturday evening with Roland Bainton's *Here I Stand* under my arm and thinking I was on the verge of an intellectual adventure. Only now in these past days have I discovered that his biography of Luther originated in lectures delivered in the immediate aftermath of the Second World War to theology students at Yale and Hartford seminaries where I have been working.[2] In a way that I can only describe as serendipitous, the conversations I have shared combined with the bridge crossing have released a flurry of competing ideas inside my head. Before coming away I was aware that English Heritage had established a pressure group

like me
taught by Dr Leslie
WHYPER.

called 'History Matters'. At the launch Stephen Fry, David Starkey and Bill Bryson had all stressed 'the vital importance of Britain's consideration of her past in the contemplation of her present and future'[3] in a context where a serious understanding of history is not greatly encouraged. The difficulty here is not just that religious people are as confused or complacent as anyone else concerning the past; it has also to do with the fact that a rapidly changing world sets most of the agenda of our lives. To paraphrase Bill Gates, his employees at the Microsoft Corporation do not drive with their eyes on the rear mirror.

My final-year students at Yale would have some sympathy with this view. They were ready to discuss the finer points of historical theology but their main concern was how their training would equip them to minister to the communities they were about to serve. They seemed most interested in theology that was 'written in blood', wrought from deep personal experience and fashioned in the here and now of the world's joys and sorrows. I told them that my own ordination card requesting prayers for my future ministry a generation ago had contained the following words of Martin Luther: 'One does not become a theologian simply by reading and studying but rather by conflict, temptation, being condemned, dying and living.' I have tried to honour this text over the years and it resonated with particular force this morning as I read the headlines of *The New York Times*. Such a theological stance on the streets of this vibrant yet unrelenting city would require, among other things, the provision of a homeless shelter for transgendered male youth prostitutes who sell their bodies to other men who want quick sex with men who look like women.[4]

The here and now is where it's at. The case for engaging with the issues, confusions and possibilities of contemporary culture without nostalgic regrets for the certainties of past times was reinforced in two other quarters beyond the Yale campus. Following a meeting with the Revd Bill McD. Tully, Rector of St Bartholomew's – a prominent mid-town Manhattan church surrounded by the glass and steel citadels of commercial America – I was struck by two things. His church is involved in a remarkable range of activities that caters for many human needs and touches the lives of those beyond the congregation. There was clear evidence of compassion, imagination and a radical openness to questions and concerns. The church stands as an open door for the poor, homeless and hungry and each week assists more than 600 people. What particularly caught my attention, however, (and this will not surprise you in view of the previous paragraph) was the organizing of regular lunchtime meetings to reflect theologically on the leading stories in *The New York Times*. The group has a Bible in one hand, so to speak, and the newspaper in the other. Topicality shapes its deliberations combined with the need to understand the complexity of a 24/7 world. It does not live in the past. Similarly, at an earlier meeting with Zvi Galil, Dean of Engineering and Applied Science at Columbia University, New York, to celebrate his new appointment as President of Tel Aviv University, I was told that he encourages his students to have some understanding of earlier centuries but impresses upon them even more the necessity of appreciating the technological achievements that are already shaping the direction of the twenty-first century. As a transformational leader and a keen runner (often with students at his side) he is driven by the search for new ideas. Terms like 'revolutionary' and 'unparalleled' represent part of his working vocabulary. He is running towards a future bright with new opportunities and challenges. The past does not detain him unduly.

I enjoyed these conversations and want to endorse the concerns that underpin them, particularly as part of my own work entails the regeneration of local urban communities. It matters that ordinary people can enjoy habitable and hopeful surroundings that enable them to believe in tomorrow. I too am a believer in such possibilities. But I also believe, no less passionately, in the past. I shall say why a little later: before then I need to recount some of the other encounters that have formed part of my recent itinerary. At an interfaith meeting in Hartford, Robert Fishman, Executive Director, Jewish Federation, Association of Connecticut, told me about his trip to Washington DC the day before to lobby politicians on the issue of immigration and refugees in his home State. Currently their disputed status denies them the educational advantages open to other local citizens. He regarded this as a clear injustice and one more example of short-term political thinking to appease a small but vindictive element of the electorate. It was also unjust because such a policy was challenged by the precepts of his religion and its insistence over a long history that peace must always be linked to justice. The prophets of old still spoke across the centuries.[5]

Later that day I shared a teaching assignment with Rabbi Dr Herb Brockman, who leads the congregation Mishkan Israel in Hamden, Connecticut. He too had been in Washington DC leading a delegation of young people concerned with environmental issues. He gave me a copy of a reworking of the Ten Commandments that in contemporary language conveyed what the delegates wished to share with policy makers. In each case the modern version was prefixed by its ancient equivalent given to Moses on the mountain at Sinai: 'Remember the Sabbath day and keep it holy' became 'Remember and respect the holiness of creation, You shall not pollute to preserve life. Allow the Earth to replenish itself'. The eighth commandment, 'You shall not steal', translated into 'Give back to the Earth what is hers. What you take return'. Old truths assumed new guises and proved serviceable for the aspirations of an emerging generation. The religious past was still able to speak to present concerns.

It was a privilege to meet these religious leaders: quite apart from their intelligence and conviction they were engaging personalities. We shared an evening meal together with Herb Brockman and other friends in an Indian restaurant. As he said over the poppadams 'no meeting without eating' – a reminder of the importance of food and conversation within Judaism. We spoke of many things: books, films, politics, the Middle East and the Vietnam War. He had served with distinction in Vietnam as a chaplain ministering to soldiers of all faiths as they fought in that ill-fated campaign. In an unguarded moment I asked him if there was a particular film about Vietnam that stood out above the rest. He replied that he had never watched any of the films about the war as the reality had been so much worse than the disturbing images portrayed on the screen. A military past that almost certainly for him contained a measure of horror had not been excised from his mind. It was still firmly embedded as part of his mental furniture and his present experience.

My final meeting, for my purposes here, was the most unexpected. It had not been scheduled in the diary and came about through a suggestion that I might like to meet Professor Ramsay MacMullen from the Department of History at Yale University. I had just read his most recent book and as he lived close by to where I was staying in New Haven, my host, John Lang, thought it would be an easy matter to drop by, say hello and have my copy personally signed by the author. We met outside his home, he autographed the book and we talked amicably for a few moments. Mission accomplished, or so I thought. My host, who was with me, then suggested to the professor that he might like to join us for lunch with two other colleagues. With commendable alacrity, the invitation was accepted and minutes later we were in deep conversation over a dining table.

The professor's book explores how the early Christian doctrines of the first five centuries came to be formulated.[6] It was a turbulent period in the history of the Church and its controversies are well documented. I have some of the classic texts on my shelves with many passages carefully underlined in red ink.[7] These books constituted part of the intellectual adventure I mentioned earlier and were studied during the formative years of my ministry in Birkenhead. Alongside the private griefs, unexpected pastoral responsibilities and various community initiatives responding to social unrest and the high levels of unemployment associated with the Thatcher years[8] that consumed most of my waking hours, it still seemed right to grapple with the Christian past.

The ecumenical councils from 325–553 AD[9] and the leading theological figures associated with them began to register more deeply than ever before and helped me to grow and survive in a context where much was asked of me. Unlike the Catholic biblical scholar, Ronald Knox, it would be too much to claim that when I couldn't sleep I would lie awake and think about the past. But I did begin to sense more acutely that 'Christianity is not one of the great things of history; history is one of the great things of Christianity'.[10]

My hunch is that Professor MacMullen would endorse this remark but not without a measure of irony. His latest research has shifted the focus of his work as a specialist in the early centuries of the Church. He has deliberately bypassed the intricacies of doctrinal debate and the politics and major personalities that influenced the meetings of the great councils and concentrated instead on what Americans would probably call 'the little guys' – the delegates who participated in church council decisions and without whom no view could claim defining authority. In his own words it 'is the whole contributing mass'[11] that he wants to understand – the many who are nothing but names to us and, quite likely, were no more than names among their fellow delegates. Looking into their minds he detects four discrete elements: a democratic, a cognitive, a supernaturalist and a violent. In each of the four he argues that there is something of major historical significance to be discovered.

It is a fascinating book but I found myself particularly drawn to the chapter dealing with the violent element. I was aware from my earlier reading of the disruptions and antagonisms that accompanied theological disputes – the *odium theologicum* (theological hatred) that frequently gave rise to ill feelings. What I had not realized until now was the level of fatal casualties. Professor MacMullen estimates a total of 25,000 deaths resulting from church disputes during the two and a quarter centuries following the Council of Nicaea (325). A small minority were clergy, the rest were faces in the crowds. All met their untimely end not as a consequence of legal proceedings but as targets of fury – stabbed, burnt alive, trampled underfoot or despatched by cold steel. The election of a bishop was 'normally a source of unrest and disorder'[12] and we read in amazement of the 137 bodies left on a cathedral floor by rival parties. A bishop represented a credal point of view that might be disputed by others. He could expect opposition that in certain instances would lead to his removal or exile. The creed that he upheld could be the determining factor that led to street fights and physical violence. Even when allowance is made for the infiltration of outside agitators or hired thugs, the fact remains that Christians, in defence of orthodoxy or fear of heresy, were ready to punch, stab and beat each other to death. A new bishop is attacked by his archdeacon; believers are encouraged to assault unbelievers and crowds are incited to hysteria:

> In all such scenes we see determined, energetic, articulate men in charge. They are willing to take risks to gain their ends; are good at judging crowd reactions; are sure they are right . . . They were indeed successful in generating the strongest feelings, capable of breaking all restraints and challenging authority.[13]

Doctrine became a desperate and deadly business and many people died or were prepared to declare each other accursed as they clashed over the nature and person of Christ. I put the book down a 'sadder and wiser man' – dismayed on the one hand by *the scale* of violence and fury and aware on the other of the grim irony contained in the earlier quotation that designated history as one of the remarkable aspects of Christianity. Professor MacMullen proved an urbane, witty and charming lunch guest. I am left contemplating the warmth of our conversation and the severe truths unearthed by his research that find a frightening parallel in the current sectarian violence in Iraq and in the long-standing hatreds between Shias and Sunnis.[14]

Some sort of tentative conclusion is called for at this point. You will not be surprised if I continue to insist that past and present need to be held together in the journey of faith. Everything I have recounted here supports such a creative partnership. The past 'is a foreign country' but it is *our* past and, from a religious perspective, it is an article of faith that Christians of every generation are bound together in a mystical sense in the Body of Christ. The past is able to feed us and surprise us and Church history, like history in general, draws us 'into a process of questioning and being questioned by the past'.[15] Like theology and philosophy the study of history constitutes a moral undertaking, an exercise in truth-seeking and a preparedness on our part to take nothing for granted as we contemplate the lives and events that in unexpected and sometimes shocking ways represent a religious response or a call to be faithful that is identical to our own. Our duty, so to speak, is to negotiate with the dead and to learn from their prayer and piety as well as their power struggles what it means to undertake the work of Christ in our time.

I can think immediately of three reasons why we might shirk this duty. Those of a conservative temper presume to know the past, therefore it holds no surprises for them and there is no negotiation to undertake. Church history is an old familiar story and its very familiarity brings the balm of reassurance. Voices are lifted high in praise and hymns are sung fervently as they recount a supposed golden age of 'One Church, One Faith, One Lord'. Progressives on the other hand, following the example of Microsoft employees, tend to have no reverse gear, which is to say that the past forms no part of their agenda. Consequently 'they do not expect to be interested or questioned by it'[16] and run the risk of making an idol of the present. The third category is harder to define and probably consists of people who fall in love with the beauty of holiness and the romance of the Christian past in such a way that its strange and forbidding elements tend not to trouble them unduly. A history, however, populated only by saints, martyrs and troubadours, and worship that brings heaven down to earth may delight heart and imagination without ever identifying what the Church *distinctively* is beyond its worship and, sadly, its divisions.

From time to time I have recognized this third tendency in myself. I have sought and found spiritual truth in all forms of beauty including the Christian religion. Even as a junior chorister, the psalms exercised a powerful hold on my imagination and an anthem that could tell of a God who would 'wipe away every tear from their eyes' (Rev. 21.4) was committed to memory and has helped to shape the person I have become. Other factors came into play later, however, that prevented my imagination from becoming mere flights of fancy. My curiosity about the past eventually assumed more rigour and the duty of critical thinking in relation to my beliefs and assumptions extended to my understanding of history. Put simply, I really wanted to know about Christian origins in order to distinguish truth from the sentimental or nostalgic. Some words of John Henry Newman registered with particular force:

> Really know what you say you know: know what you know and what you do not know: get one thing well before you go on to a second; try to ascertain what your words mean; when you read a sentence picture it before your mind as a whole, take in the truth or information contained in it, express it in your own words, and, if it be important, commit it to the faithful memory. Again, compare one idea with another; adjust truths and facts; form them into one whole, or notice the obstacles which occur in doing so. This is the way to make progress; this is the way to arrive at results; not to swallow knowledge . . . but to digest it.[17]

For Newman this is one of the ways that faith is safe-guarded and protected from bigotry and fanaticism. But it can also act as a corrective to slipshod ways of thinking about the past that evade the labour of hard thought which makes for spiritual growth and vision. In his *Confessions*, Augustine imagines God encouraging us to 'Grow and feed upon me'.[18] Our reading of history makes possible such nurture but not if we *think* foolishly[19] or, for that matter, sing unreflectively as we chant along with the choir in praise of things past. Here is another eminent Victorian, the novelist and poet Thomas Hardy, calling to mind remembered afternoons in the village church of the mid-nineteenth century:

> On afternoons of drowsy calm
> We stood in the panelled pew,
> Singing one-voiced a Tate-and-Brady psalm
> To the tune of 'Cambridge New'.
>
> We watched the elms, we watched the rooks
> The clouds upon the breeze,
> Between the whiles of glancing at our books,
> And swaying like the trees.
>
> So mindless were those outpourings! –
> Though I am not aware
> That I have gained by subtle thought on things
> Since we stood psalming there.[20]

The exclamation mark and that uncompromising word 'mindless' are highly revealing: we are spirited back to occasions of piety marked by an absence of devotion and a parroting of formulaic verse. Despite the agnosticism and unbelief of Hardy's later years and the 'subtle thought' that no longer gave him joy or certitude,[21] he continued to value the rituals of church life – 'it was good for people to get clean and come together once a week'[22] – but disliked religious cant and the vapid thought that frequently accompanied it.[23]

There is a line of argument that wishes to defend such language as harmless: after all, most of us rely to some degree on received wisdom, and without commonplace assumptions our conversations with God or each other would become stilted, unintelligible or even mute. Whether in worship or the work-place there is comfort and utility in familiar modes of speech and as Rorty reminded us in an earlier chapter, they help us to cope with a perplexing world. Against this, however, has to be set the danger of the foolish thinking or 'vain repetition' that rarely penetrate the past and therefore make of it 'a mirror for our own preferences and assumptions'.[24] Hardy lived a long reflective life, clear in his mind to the end, with a knowledge of the past 'like a man who has lived more than one span of life'.[25]

In that last phrase lies the value of our study of history and our negotiation with the dead. They hold out to us the possibility of straddling the generations of believers who, in ways we have barely realized, have made us what we are. To engage with the Christian past is to be astonished by habits of thought and behaviour that by turn seem attractive, holy, alien or hostile to our own contemporary understanding yet are still recognizably part of the trajectory of faith that binds us to the witnesses of the earliest centuries. Our identity as Christians is enriched because of our heightened awareness that some sort of conversation is still possible across the centuries and the wide gaps in context and understanding between one age and another. In terms of faith this is to grasp that we are not the first pilgrims and to recognize this almost, as it were, for the first time.

To begin to know something of our origins in such a way that they come to represent more than an impressionistic or vague sequence of events that frequently conceal more than they disclose is to be granted a particular kind of wisdom.[26] By this I mean the realism which does not resort to a sly cynicism about the past,[27] refuses to view Christian history solely in terms of glory or shame and knows, really knows, if only a little, about the forces, sometimes benevolent or sublime, often political and occasionally malign, that have contributed to the faith we seek to live by. By really knowing about the internal violence that was integral to the religious controversies of the early centuries we begin to understand rather better that the dark materials of Christianity have a long history and retain a frightening capacity to reconfigure themselves in new forms with the passage of time. In consequence I am not surprised to learn that when an itinerant black preacher named William J. Seymour arrived in Los Angeles a century ago, blind in one eye, scarred by smallpox but filled with a love for God and a desire to embrace people of every colour in his makeshift church on Azusa Street, he was reviled by local fundamentalist Christians, one of whom described him as 'The last vomit of Satan'.[28] I recoil from these words because they appear utterly alien to the mandate of Christ that we should love one another (Jn. 15.17) and serve to remind me that the plague of religious intolerance never dies or disappears for good. To echo some words of Albert Camus writing of another and equally deadly form of pestilence: 'It can lie dormant for years and years in furniture and linen chests . . . it bides its time in bedrooms, cellars, trunks and bookshelves.'[29]

This is not the true religion that I have come to associate with the 'great cloud of witnesses' attested to in Hebrews – a company that through my reading of history now appears to me as something real and durable rather than a sentimental abstraction. I know, really know, for example, that when the Church sullied the radiant face of its Lord with its tantrums, divisions and death-dealing, something else was going on that was more redemptive and Christ-like. My authority here is Newman, writing in 1859 of the failure of bishops and Councils as they spoke against one another after Nicaea: 'There was nothing of firm, unvarying consistent testimony for nearly sixty years. There was weakness, misguidance, delusion, hallucination, endless, hopeless, extending itself into nearly every corner of the Catholic Church.'[30] But as the episcopate was unfaithful to its commission, it was the body of the laity – 'the Christian people under Providence'[31] – that maintained the Church in truth, became a source of strength to others and was faithful in its prayers and witness. At a time when the truth of Christ was in danger of being obscured or concealed, it was necessary, Newman argued, to 'have recourse to the faithful in order to know the tradition of the Apostles'.[32]

Most of these faithful lives left no indelible mark on the world and were soon forgotten. Like us, they believed, had wandering thoughts from time to time, probably found the going hard yet persevered and prayed. We have an epitaph found in Asia Minor during the fourth century that reads: 'Here sleeps the blessed Chione, who has found Jerusalem for she prayed much'.[33] We know nothing more about her but it is enough to know that she represents all those who, in quiet and unspectacular ways, held fast to Christ during a time of pestilence.

I have surprised myself with this chapter. It has unfolded in a way that I had not anticipated and a quite different narrative has emerged instead of the more prosaic contents originally planned for these pages. I am glad about this, and in relation to what I have tried to say here let me finally share with you some words of Austin Farrer, a great Anglican theologian of the last century, who was blessed with an abundance of brains and a truth-seeking heart:

> After all the detection of shams, the clarification of argument, and the sifting of evidence – after all criticism, all analysis – a man must make up his mind what there is most worthy of love, and most binding on conduct in the world of real existence. It is this decision, or this discovery, that is the supreme exercise of a truth-seeking intelligence.[34]

Faith is about decision and discovery and the need to make up our minds concerning how we ought to live. History can be our guide and has much to offer us by way of practical wisdom. But we must not think foolishly in relation to the Christian past. If we are committed to the business of truth-seeking we should be prepared to dig.

5

A World Elsewhere:
the Elusive Kingdom

When Jesus sends out the Twelve to preach the gospel
of the kingdom he instructs them to travel lightly.
They are to take 'nothing for the journey' as they
travel through the villages of the region and they are
to rely on the hospitality of those who receive them
(Lk. 9.1–6). Now that I am back from America it
occurs to me that my recent trip fulfilled two of these
requirements but failed miserably in one important
respect. Like the apostles, I moved around from place
to place (for villages read towns and cities!) and having performed my duties waited upon the kindness of
strangers. In keeping with previous visits I am happy
to report that I received the warmest of welcomes.
This partly explains the affection I retain for America
and why I sometimes find myself in the role of 'go
between', trying to interpret one nation to another
when the conversation clearly reveals some basic mis-
understandings. I have just come across the following
advice given by Sir Christopher Meyer, our former
Ambassador in Washington, to new recruits at the
British Embassy:

> The core of my message was always the same:
> think of the US as a foreign country; then you
> will be pleasantly surprised by the many

things you find in common with this most
generous and hospitable of peoples. Think
of America as Britain writ large and you
risk coming to grief; American attitudes to
patriotism, religion, crime and punishment,
schooling, sex, the outside world, can be very
different from those of Europeans including
the British. For the novice British diplomat it
comes as a shock to discover that most Americans, whether Republican or Democratic,
sophisticate or redneck, believe that their
country's actions in the world are intrinsically virtuous; and more fool those countries
that do not recognise this. The attitude of
Britain's Victorians was very similar.[1]

Much of this rings true to my experience and the
ostensible 'special relationship' between Britain and
America would improve overnight if the Ambassador's advice found its way inside every UK pass-
port! I shall return to his remarks later after I have
confessed my signal shortcoming as a twenty-first
century apostle. In marked contrast to the instruction of Jesus to move about easily without the burden
of baggage, I returned home with more luggage than
when I set out! Souvenirs and duty-free took up very
little extra space but the main problem was where to
pack the extra books that had, somewhat predictably,
multiplied over the weeks. Some of these were gifts
gratefully received, others the inevitable outcome of
forays into Broadway bookstores that held me captive for several hours. There was also a selection
of academic texts that I had agreed to review for a
theological journal, including the edited writings
of Austin Farrer,[2] praised in the last chapter for his
outstanding gifts as priest, pastor and teacher. In the

third chapter of *The Glass of Vision* (first published in 1948) he suggests that the thought and teaching of Christ and St Paul are expressed most powerfully in images. Jesus speaks enigmatically of the Son of Man, of Israel as the human family of God, of bread and wine as tokens of sacrifice and communion, of the sower who went out to sow. And he intrigues and baffles his listeners by his frequent references to the kingdom of God that constitute the central theme of his message (Matt. 4.17, 23; Mk. 1.15; Lk. 4.42, 43). In total there are some 50 sayings and parables of Jesus that relate to the kingdom and as a first-century Palestinian Jew he would have been aware that his own Hebrew scriptures set forth a hope in God's ultimate disclosure as king. Jesus adopts this language, makes it his own and in his preaching declares that in some sense the kingdom is to be identified in his own presence, and in some other sense is still to be anticipated and prayed for. We feel for his followers when he goes on to say that some of them will still be alive when God's rule is firmly established (Matt. 16.28). Not only are they perplexed by this teaching, they face the need to repent and make their lives all over again. And they must begin this work of transformation now, for the climax of history is much nearer than they realize.

Farrer writes elegantly and persuasively on this theme and it is hard to resist the prominence of the kingdom in the gospels.[3] Trading on his wisdom, I have often drawn students and groups into debate by making a sharp distinction between Jesus and Paul in order to distinguish what the gospel is about and to what, therefore, we are called to surrender our lives. My opening shot usually rests on a provocative sound bite: 'the proclaimer became the proclaimed'. In other words, whereas Jesus preached about the kingdom, Paul and the other apostles preached the gospel of Gethsemane and Golgotha. There is a switch of emphasis away from the future reign of God to the word of the cross: 'For Jews demand signs and Greeks desire wisdom, but we proclaim Christ crucified, a stumbling-block to Jews and foolishness to Gentiles, but to those who are the called, both Jews and Greeks, Christ the power of God and the wisdom of God.' (1 Cor. 1.22–24). Paul is in combative mood: all that it is necessary for us to know is the truth of Christ and we come to know this through our identification with his death (2 Cor. 4.7–11). My sound bite succeeds in provoking discussion but like all slogans it is not the whole truth. Farrar, remember, is wanting us to see how images are used by Jesus *and Paul* as a means of revelation. But, actually, when it is Paul under consideration do we not tend to view him as a complicated thinker trading concepts and ideas, arguing wherever he can get a hearing and setting down in a systematic way the principles which his readers are to live by?[4] Far from his thought being centred round images it seems to move in the opposite direction, casting him instead in the role of *image breaker* – a theological iconoclast determined that old ways of thinking about the law of God, the nature of faith and the way to human freedom must be broken if the true gospel, with its promise of a new creation, is to replace error and distortions.[5]

I confess that for a while this was how I saw Paul. But the scholarship of Farrer and others[6] has drawn me to the mystical dimension of the apostle's teaching and I now see how 'his own life in Christ is a continual death and resurrection',[7] in, and of itself, an image of the strange man on the cross. Paul's mind and writings are shaped by such images: the suffering Son, Christ the obedient servant, the crucified God, the exalted Lord, the faithful Abraham, the old and new Israel, the life-giving Spirit, the cosmic Christ in whom all things were created – all these and more inform the consuming vision that he longs to share with others. At the end of an extraordinary life and ministry that set the western world on a new trajectory he is brought to Rome under guard and lives there for two years or more. His passion for Christ and his love of argument remain undiminished and great numbers come to his lodgings to debate with him (Acts 28.23–24). He tries to convince them about Jesus, drawing on the law of Moses and the prophets to advance his case. But this is not his only concern. During his waking hours he welcomes visitors and – how did I miss this? – he testifies to the kingdom of God! The Scriptures do not disclose his future to us, they say only that he lives at his own expense and speaks openly and unhindered about the kingdom (Acts 28.30–31). We are given no dates and times concerning its coming. We are left instead with an image that speaks of hope and conviction, of impossible yet tantalizing dreams, of a world elsewhere and a longing (such a deep and uniquely human longing) that the justice, peace and love of heaven should come down to renew the face of a world where the serpent still beguiles and destroys (Gen. 3.13, 23–24) and where the poor and meek have no immediate prospect of inheriting the earth (Matt. 5.3, 5).

As I reflect more carefully on these closing verses of Acts, I find myself working with not one but two images. The kingdom, of course, but also the endearing picture of Paul in the winter of his years. I have allowed my imagination to work on this passage, partly because the poetry of William Blake has been my bedtime reading for the past few nights. In a letter to Dr Trusler dated 23 August 1799 Blake notes that the reason why 'the Bible is more entertaining and instructive than any other book'[8] is because it is addressed to the imagination – the human faculty that for Blake was more important than understanding or reason. He had the sublime gift of being able to see 'the infinite in all things' and it is through the imagination that we begin to build Jerusalem and see within the Scriptures the hand of God. For this to happen we need to pause so that we can glimpse the mystery that lies beyond the words. When the French poet and mystic, Charles Péguy, published his first poem on Joan of Arc, his readers were puzzled and in some cases annoyed to find among the pages of text a number which were entirely blank. It was not a printer's error but a deliberate choice on the part of Péguy: the blanks gave his readers time to be silent before hurrying on.[9]

As I pause in order to see Paul, a description of him from the second century comes to mind: 'He was a man of small stature with a bald head and bow legs. His eyebrows met in the middle. His nose was rather large and he was full of grace for at times he seemed like a man and at times he had the face of an angel.'[10] I love the ambivalence of this image reflecting, as it does, the mercurial, difficult and godly apostle, who displays so many different guises and temperaments as we encounter him through his letters. He has more time now that his travels are over, more opportunity for the searching life of prayer that he commends to others as the hallmark of our conversation with Christ.[11] Free from the crowd he works and prays, quietly setting down sublime words that will not be forgotten.[12] He has never really cared whether he lives or dies – not since the great cause of the gospel first claimed his allegiance – and all that finally matters to him is that we should become more Christlike and more open to the creative love and grace of God (Phil. 2.5–13).

Here is the first clue to unravelling the secret of the kingdom. It has to begin with us and the recognition that the change we wish to see in a world scarred by cruelty, poverty and injustice must also address the shadows and darkness within us. Until we have grappled with the wayward desires that so easily mar human nature, our belief that a perfect world is just around the corner will never move beyond the sentimental or self-deluded. Paul is a realist about the morass of our inner lives that frequently blights good intentions. He knows from his own experience that at some deep level we are alienated from God. There can be no genuinely good life for ourselves or others until we know who and where we are. Before we can save the rainforest we must also learn to save ourselves. I am old enough to recall the famous Children's Crusade of America in the 1960s, summed up by Jerry Rubin, whose futuristic credo amounted to this:

> There will be no more jails, no courts or police. The White House will become a crash pad for anybody without a place to stay in Washington.
>
> The world will be one big commune with free food and housing, everything shared. Barbers will go to rehabilitation camps where they will grow their hair long. There will be no more schools or churches because the entire world will become one church and school.[13]

The manifesto is not without humour – I particularly

like the line about barbers relinquishing their trade and letting their locks grow! But I doubt that I found it entirely convincing even as I sang along with my generation about the dawning of the Age of Aquarius. Rubin's radicalism was a deeply contrived thing that predictably guaranteed him 15 minutes of fame. More tellingly, however, it never contemplated the possibility that real revolution should concern itself with the recalcitrant habits of the heart as well as social structures. We were told there would be no jails, no courts, no police, no schools, no churches, because sweet reason and a spirit of universal brotherhood would sweep everything before them and 'the entire world will become one church and school'.[14] What we were not told about was our own need to be restored, healed and forgiven before we could become the means of grace and love to others. Such a consecrated life made no sense to Rubin; for Paul, by contrast, it meant everything if we are to remain committed to the long revolution that represents our journey from bondage to the freedom that is to be found in 'the kingdom of God's beloved Son' (Col. 1.13).

Something else follows from this identification of the kingdom with the death and resurrection of Christ. Even now in small but significant ways the transformation of all things can begin: ordinary lives touched by the Spirit can become outposts of the kingdom in which God's will might be realized through the reordering of human relationships that are no longer to be determined by worldly concerns but are instead to grow 'to the full stature of Christ' (Eph. 4.14). To be clear: for Paul the kingdom of God is inseparable from the *person of Christ*.

When faith is challenged to make a stand, or is required to give its allegiance to a cause that will

settle for nothing less than the submission of hearts
and minds to a person or movement, it will be right
to ask: 'Where is the mind of Christ in this?' The
earlier remark of Sir Christopher Meyer concerning
the tendency of the American people to believe in the
essential righteousness of their nation is not without
its dangers. The Great Seal of the United States shows
a pyramid inscribed with the year 1776, rising above
an arid desert. Above the pyramid the inscription (in
Latin) reads 'God has favoured our undertakings'.
Below, another Latin phrase announces 'a new order
of the ages'. The American Founding Fathers, along
with prominent theologians and writers, saw *the
nation* as the embodiment of the City of God and
a symbol of a newly found innocence. A new Israel
had been born and in the figure of George Washington, the country had its Saviour. Many Americans
virtually deified him and Washington was equally
adamant that the hand of heaven was guiding his
endeavours.[15] God was on the side of a nation that
could do no wrong; its destiny was assured and to
this end even Christ could be reduced to the role of
teacher rather than the Son of God to whom, according to Paul, 'thrones, dominions, rulers and powers'
(Col. 1.16) are all accountable.[16] At least America had
its 'checks and balances' and the inevitable leanings
towards triumphalism were tempered by voices which
insisted that God's will and purposes were far more
mysterious than anyone had realized and certainly
not to be wholly identified with the great American
story as pioneers pushed further westward.[17]

History tends to repeat itself. A little more than 50
years after the American Civil War, extreme German
nationalism combined with anti-Semitism began to
speak of a kingdom that would last a thousand years

with all the trappings of a State religion and to which the German Church would be subordinated as a *de facto* instrument of the Nazi party. In a time of great moral darkness many spiritual leaders capitulated. Others represented the voice of Christian conscience, protesting against the persecution of the Jews and the undermining of fundamental Christian principles. Drawing on the New Testament Karl Barth and Dietrich Bonhoeffer, assisted by other Confessing Church leaders, issued the famous Theological Declaration of Barmen in 1934.[18] The Declaration rejected the idea that the State 'could become the single and totalitarian order of human life' and the accompanying notion that Christ and his kingdom could be reduced to 'any arbitrarily chosen desires, purposes and plans'. At a critical moment the German Evangelical Church preferred Christ to the rule of the Nazis, seeing in him 'God's mighty claim upon our whole life' and living solely 'from his comfort and his direction'. The spirit of Paul animates the document: the Church is a society of pardoned sinners and the template of its shared life is the obedience of faith predicated on a kingdom represented by the One whom 'we have to trust and obey in life and in death'.

The courage epitomized by the Declaration of Barmen represents an impressive story that prevented the apostasy of the Church in a tragic period of its history. God was not left without his witnesses and his kingdom resisted the pernicious and evil doctrines that equated a new world order with the deification of Hitler, 'the religion of the blood' and the extermination of a race of people. A kingdom of the racially pure would carry all before it. Difference would be rooted out and destroyed in the name of the ersatz religion of National Socialism and its racial creed. Paul would have neither understood nor tolerated any of this. We know that he was a formidable opponent when views contrary to his own infiltrated his communities[19] but he was also capable of tolerance (1 Cor. 7.6–7) and true friendship (Rom. 16.1–6) that extended to all. The fact is, many people were drawn to him. At the end of his sojournings the crowds keep coming to his door to hear him because this difficult, deeply human and endearing ambassador for Christ is *for* them, not *against* them. These are his own people (Rom. 9.3) and if necessary he is even prepared to be excluded – 'to be cut off' (Rom. 9.3) – from the incomparable joy of Christ for their sake. My hunch is that few of us really grasp the extent and depth of Paul's concern here. Even before his arrival in Rome he has responded to the anti-Jewish feeling that is rife among the Roman aristocracy and beginning to infect the Christian community. There has been a recent anti-Jewish pogrom in Alexandria (38–41) and even more recent tax riots in nearby Puteoli, resulting in deaths. He is also anxious about the welfare of a vulnerable minority Jewish population in the imperial capital that has already suffered expulsion from the city by the emperor Claudius around 49 AD. They are Paul's people and God's children – 'there is no distinction between Jew and Greek' (Rom. 10.12) – and with God differences of race and gender no longer count. In warning his readers of the dangers of arrogance or hostility towards the Jews (Rom. 11.13–36) he testifies to a kingdom that is open and hospitable: its gates stand welcoming for the Lord 'is generous to all who call upon him' (Rom. 10.12), especially the needy and poor.[20] Paul has already tasted the fruits of Zion that symbolize the 'new covenant' of Jesus (Heb. 12.22) and he has never failed to carry the burdens of the brokenhearted (Gal. 6.2). But now, with his life almost poured out, he is prepared to be denied the promise and glory vouchsafed to all the saints, if this means that others may share in such a hope. For the sake of his people, he will set aside the pearl of great price (Matt. 13.46) and the prize 'of the heavenly call of God in Christ Jesus' (Phil. 3.14). But I, for one, cannot imagine the kingdom without him. As the picture fades I am cheered and encouraged by the sight of this extraordinary apostle in his final days, pointing the hearts and minds of those who will hear to the bright day of God's justice and a world where righteousness shall prevail.

It seems to me that faith cannot be sustained without such a vision and must continually draw strength from it. When we have done our best, only to realize that there is still much darkness within and without, we do not lose heart. To believe in Christ's kingdom is to speak audaciously of hope and to work with others for its fulfilment.[21] The dream of all things being made new in Christ and a kingdom where the persecuted and peacemakers are blessed (Matt. 5.9–10) often seems far from us yet, on other days, we feel its closeness. It continues to feed our moral imagination and has survived the prejudice and oppression of lesser kingdoms that constitute our human stain. Close to my hand as I write this is a recent obituary of Jim Clark, sheriff and segregationist from Alabama, who has died aged 84. Back in the early 1960s he dressed like a soldier as he got ready for a day's work. He had the swagger of a big man – weighing 16 stone and more than six feet tall – and he carried a truncheon, rope and cattle prod along with a .38 calibre pistol. He wore a sheriff's star and a small white lapel button which announced boldly: 'Never'. Never, that

is, 'to let the niggers overcome him'. The cattle prod
was useful to marshal black people 'of low IQ' who
believed they should have the right to vote. He was
famous for beating Negroes and once made 165 teen-
agers run out of town and carry on running, 'mile
after mile, prod after prod',[22] until they were sick
with exhaustion. To ladies in white gloves and hats
he epitomized charm; to the blacks who continually
lined up to register to vote at the courthouse steps he
could be relied on to behave arrogantly and, if necessary, brutally. His town, Selma, had been identified
by a Baptist church leader as the most segregated
town in the country with only 1 per cent of its blacks
registered to vote. On 28 August 1963, this young
black minister assembled near the Lincoln Memorial
in Washington DC with 250,000 people to rally for
jobs, freedom and civil rights. Speakers representing
different facets of American society were each allot-
ted 15 minutes: they included Sydney Poitier, Marlon
Brando and Joan Baez. The minister's turn to speak
arrived and his intention was to recite the sufferings
of African-Americans still struggling for freedom in
a society disfigured by discrimination. But the gospel
singer Mahalia Jackson shouted out: 'Tell them about
your dream, Martin! Tell them about the dream!' The
crowd became animated and Dr Martin Luther King
Jr. gave the speech that has passed into history. He
spoke of 'the Negro's legitimate discontent' and the
need to 'lift our nation from the quicksands of racial
injustice to the solid rock of brotherhood'. And then,
responding to the shouts of the audience, he declaimed
the politics of paradise:

> I say to you today, my friends . . . so even
> though we face the difficulties of today and
> tomorrow, I still have a dream. It is a dream

deeply rooted in the American dream. I have a dream that one day this nation will rise up and live out the true meaning of its creed: 'We hold these truths to be self-evident: that all men are created equal.' I have a dream that one day on the red hills of Georgia the sons of former slaves and the sons of former slave owners will be able to sit down together at the table of brotherhood. I have a dream that one day even the state of Mississippi, a state sweltering with the heat of injustice, sweltering with the heat of oppression, will be transformed into an oasis of freedom and justice. I have a dream that my four little children will one day live in a nation where they will not be judged by the color of their skin but by the content of their character. I have a dream today. I have a dream that one day, down in Alabama, with its vicious racists, with its governor having his lips dripping with the words of interposition and nullification; one day right there in Alabama, little black boys and black girls will be able to join hands with little white boys and white girls as sisters and brothers. I have a dream today. I have a dream that one day every valley shall be exalted, every hill and mountain shall be made low, the rough places will be made plain, and the crooked places will be made straight, and the glory of the Lord shall be revealed, and all flesh shall see it together.[23]

Under an almost cloudless sky, a prophetic voice was heard in the land, speaking with the tongue of an angel yet utterly resolute concerning the reality of oppression and the audacious faith that would, one day 'transform the jangling discords of our nation into a beautiful symphony of brotherhood'. Former President Bill Clinton records in his autobiography that he cried when he listened to this speech at the age of 17 and Gordon Brown has recently included Dr King in a series of portraits of human courage.[24] King drew strength and inspiration from a range of sources. He had studied the theology of Paul Tillich and had been drawn to his idea of unconditional love. He was familiar with the writings of Reinhold Niebuhr who, with an almost forensic precision, had unmasked 'the glaring reality of collective evil'.[25] He was also drawn to the teachings of Gandhi concerning non-violent resistance. More than anything else, however, it is possible to see in the biblical imagery of, perhaps, this greatest of speeches, the influence of his preacher father at the Ebenezer church of his youth and, before that, the great line of black preachers who never relinquished the hope of 'the freedom of the glory of the children of God' (Rom. 8.21).

King believed that a nation inspired by such a vision of all God's children – 'black and white, Jews and Gentiles, Protestants and Catholics' – could still build a good and just society capable of overcoming the sinfulness of humanity. He was awarded the Nobel Peace Prize in 1964 but only four years later found himself beleaguered, convinced that 'the tide of history was flowing in a different direction'.[26] He left us with much still to be done. But not before he had turned the tide and directed us, like Jesus and Paul, to the elusive kingdom that reflects the depth and strength of an abiding dream of a world redeemed and our longing to share in it.

6

Mapping the Kingdom: Politics and the Christian Vision

About the time that Martin Luther King was lifting the eyes of the American people to a vision of a more just and free society, I too was beginning to learn a little about the meaning of the kingdom of Christ. I was in my early teens, a keen chorister and altar server in a local parish church close to the heart of Manchester. There, along with others, I had the privilege of being led by a priest who lodged thoughts in my mind that were not forgotten. Frederick William Osborn was a quiet but passionate saint who made God real. He taught me about the beauty of holiness, the importance of worship and self-discipline, the reckless nature of Christ's love and the graced lives of the saints and martyrs. From his sermons I first became aware of the courage of Dietrich Bonhoeffer. From his gentle smile, patience and hospitality – one room of his rectory was equipped with a mini snooker table for hard up choristers! – I sensed that life was bound up with service and a practical concern for others. Each Tuesday evening a small group of young people would gather in church for a short service before walking two miles with huge containers of hot soup for homeless men living in a makeshift shelter near the city centre. Fr Osborn had acquired a shop and transformed it into a home for those who had been sleeping rough. The project was featured on local television and later moved to more spacious premises where we continued to make the weekly soup run. I trace my own work in housing and homelessness over many years to those early and poignant encounters.

In the shelters I discovered how easily lives could fall apart and gradually came to see that the Christian gospel was much more than the conventional business of churchgoing or being a respectable citizen. It was a great cause extending beyond the boundaries of the Church with a special concern for the poor and forgotten. The kingdom was about compassion, keeping my life in order and staying in touch with others who came together to break bread and pray.

Eventually Fr Osborn was called to another parish. We wept as we sang 'The day thou gavest, Lord, is ended' at his final service. The church was later demolished as part of the regeneration of the area. I moved to another congregation, even closer to the city, but continued to write to my former rector. From time to time we met and he would listen as I tried to fathom what my life was for. I was now approaching 20 with the unexpected possibility of a career in personnel management. One day, at his suggestion, we met in Manchester where he introduced me to Bishop Colin Winter who, as a young man, had also been deeply influenced by our mutual friend. Over lunch I heard about the bishop's work in Namibia, the witness against apartheid in South Africa and the prophetic voice of church leaders who could not be silent in the face of the viciousness and lies that degraded people of colour at every turn. We parted and he promised that his community at Windhoek would send me regular postings. They arrived and for a short while I wondered if the Episcopal lunch and subsequent mailings were pointing me towards Africa. It was not to be. I progressed in my career and Bishop Winter was forced to leave the country and the people that he had come to love. What I was left with, however, was the realization that I could no longer think about the kingdom of God solely in terms of the Good Samaritan or my personal relationship with Christ. Along with worship, kindness to others and self-control, there was now the duty of struggle – of engagement with the political realm and the need to resist the 'rulers of this age' (1 Cor.2–8) when they denied the image of God in their people. Although I could not easily articulate it then, I sensed that politics and economics – the twin levers that contribute so massively to human flourishing, dignity or despair – were of prime importance in seeking God's kingdom. The gospel was a social gospel with a larger remit than personal relationships, individual responses and faithfulness in prayer.[1]

My second 'awakening' came on the night of 20 August 1968. The date lacks the resonance of 9/11 or the death of a Princess but for me it marked a turning point in my life and an anniversary that I have kept with every passing year. On that night as people lay sleeping, the Soviet Union and its Warsaw Pact allies invaded Czechoslovakia. Up to 7,000 tanks occupied the streets and they were followed by over 200,000 troops. Many people were killed and hundreds wounded. The Czechoslovakian leader, Alexander Dubcek, was arrested and taken to Moscow with several of his colleagues. His alleged crime was to have initiated the earlier reforms of that year that came to be known as the Prague Spring. As the new leader of the Communist Party in Czechoslovakia, Dubcek wanted freedom of the press, a more democratic multi-party government and greater access to consumer goods. His fellow communists in the USSR feared that such reforms would weaken their position during the Cold War. In the months following the invasion, Dubcek was replaced, the Spring he had initiated fell silent and the Party was purged of its liberal members. Those expressing open dissent within the professions were dismissed from their jobs. Non-violent resistance to the invasion was expressed in many ways: signs, graffiti and placards appeared everywhere. In Britain, on the night following the invasion and by a strange quirk of history, the Soviet Union Symphony Orchestra was performing the Czech-born composer Antonin Dvorak's elegiac cello concerto at the London Proms. Initial booing and hostility in the audience towards the orchestra gave way to tears as the Russian cellist, Mstislav Rostropovitch transformed the concerto into a lament for an invasion that neither he nor the orchestra knew anything of until one of its members had tuned in to a pirate radio station. On 16 January 1969 the most potent protest, by far, took place in Wenceslas Square, Prague, when Jan Palach, a young Czech student died after setting fire to himself. His funeral turned into a major demonstration against the occupation. Later, the secret police set out to destroy the memory of his deed and exhumed his remains during the night of 25 October 1973. His body was cremated and the corpse of an elderly woman from a rest home was laid in his grave. However, Palach was never forgotten by his people and he is now commemorated by a bronze cross at the place where he died outside the National Museum. A square is also named in his honour. Many years later I travelled there to pay my respects.

What did I feel and think about these upheavals at the time? First, I wanted to understand why the invasion had happened so suddenly and the nature of the events leading up to it. From 20 August I began reading a broadsheet daily newspaper and later subscribed to *The Economist* – a paper that I now think is possibly the best in the world. I studied the reaction of the western countries, the political developments behind the scenes and the *Brezhnev Doctrine* that compelled the socialist governments of the satellite states of the Soviet Union to subordinate their national interests to those of the Eastern Bloc. For the first time I recognized 'on the pulse' the brutal nature of international politics when ideologies collided and how power was exercised through the barrel of a gun. I also felt a deep sorrow for Jan Palach (the same age as myself) and the subjugation of his people. Politics was no longer a private game played in the corridors of power with little or no relevance to ordinary lives. What we make of the world, what it takes to render dignity and meaning to people's lives, what we expect or hope to see in terms of decency,[2] respect and fairness in government and human relationships – these are all profoundly religious and moral issues derived from a gospel that endorses the creation as good and the Earth as a place to be lived in and improved. To a large degree they represent the touchstones that enable us to *map the kingdom* and the extent to which love, justice and compassion are facing or overcoming obvious injustice, tyranny and fear. They also constitute the stuff of politics and how well those who lead the family of nations[3] identify with, or depart from, a vision of the common good and universal ideals. Politics, I came to see, was too important to be left to politicians when they frustrated the 'value and grandeur of the human person'⁴ and his unique dignity as a child of God.

A third 'epiphany' was still to come. Returning from America at the end of 1971 I had become increasingly preoccupied with the character and leadership of Richard Nixon, the 37ᵗʰ President of the United States. Travelling across the country, T-shirts with the slogan 'Would you buy a used car from this man?' printed underneath his face seemed to be everywhere. He was 'Tricky Dicky', not to be trusted and hated by many for needlessly and brutally prolonging a futile war in Vietnam. I was on the side of his critics. The Watergate burglary at the Democratic National Committee headquarters on 17 June 1972 and the subsequent cover-up that led to the Oval Office of the White House and showed the President to be guilty of deceit, concealment, mendacity and a shocking reluctance to face up to personal confrontations, served only to intensify my interest and disdain. After more than two years of extraordinary disclosures and investigations that I followed closely in the press, he resigned the Presidency during a live broadcast at 9.01 p.m. on 8 August 1974 to a listening audience of 150 million in the United States alone. I tuned in with millions of others around the world and in the darkness of my bedroom thrust my hand in the air as I heard the words 'Therefore I shall resign the Presidency effective at noon tomorrow.'

That should have been the end of the saga – justice done and a bad man ejected from high office. But my interest in Nixon continued to grow. I read about his early life, his voracious thirst for serious reading, his evening prayers before bed and his remarkable (to some, saintly) mother and grandmother, both

Quakers, who taught him the importance of 'peace at the centre' and compassion for the underprivileged. On his thirteenth birthday Almira (his grandmother) gave him a framed portrait of Abraham Lincoln with two verses from Longfellow's 'Psalm of Life' carefully copied in her own handwriting:

Lives of great men oft remind us
We can make our lives sublime
And departing leave behind us
Footprints on the sand of time.

Footprints that perhaps another
Sailing o'er life's stormy main
A forlorn and shipwrecked brother
Seeing may take heart again.[5]

Eight years later and perhaps still inspired by these lines Nixon wrote a series of essays as a college student under the heading 'What Can I Believe?' in which he set forth the life of Jesus as his ideal and a renewed vision of his kingdom as the means to world peace. The essays are remarkable for their seriousness and self-analysis. Asked to comment on them in 1990 without any knowledge of the identity of the original writer an Anglican Archbishop observed: 'Whoever wrote this was already at an advanced level of spirituality which could not have remained static within him. He must have risen very much higher or fallen very much lower, quite possibly both, but such strong spiritual roots would never have died and must have been very important to him.'[6]

Now, more than 10 years after Nixon's death and the ignominy of his resignation, it seems remarkable to me that, despite his misdemeanours and failings, he was also a courageous leader of vast and serious intellect and hidden depths of sensitivity and faith. In a long retirement he was forgiven by many and his contributions to the kingdom of Christ in dismantling the segregated schools of the South when no one else had been able to do it and then reaching out to China and the Soviet Union have come to be regarded as 'historic achievements by a giant of peace-making'.[7] In one of my notebooks that I carry with me I keep part of an obituary of Nixon that appeared in the *Guardian* newspaper. It is a fair assessment and includes some lines from an old Scots ballad that the disgraced President pondered as he flew back to California following his resignation: 'I am hurt, but I am not slain. I will rest and bleed awhile and then I will fight again'.[8] I have on many occasions written these words on cards and in letters to people facing personal crises. They seem to help but, inevitably, they remind me of a resilient politician and wayward pilgrim who never entirely relinquished the high ideals of his childhood or his college dream of a world 'in which peace and freedom can live together'.[9] In his eightieth year as he reflected on his early childhood, when he rose at 4.30 a.m. to wash and display vegetables in the family grocery store before catching the school bus at 8.00 a.m., he was also looking to the future, writing speeches and planning a visit to Moscow to increase US aid to Russia in the cause of peace.[10]

The complexity of Nixon's character and the strange trajectory of his political career, ranging as it did from the low political cunning and deceit that invited scorn and derision to the originality of thought and wider vision that brought him plaudits in old age, contain some important lessons for those who still believe that 'in keeping with his promise we are looking forward to a new heaven and a new earth, the home of righteousness' (2 Pet. 3.13). First, we should resist the temptation (so much greater now in an era dominated by sleaze and spin) to use the word 'politician' polemically or with a degree of disdain that is not, in principle, justified. Politicians are not by nature given only to ambition, self-interest and opportunism: as part of 'the crooked timber of humanity'[11] they are like the rest of us, prone to sinfulness but also capable of greatness and goodness. If we prick them they bleed and in their private moments they are not spared the quiet desperation that occasionally attends the lives of all ordinary citizens. It is not, I suspect, widely known that Gordon Brown's recent book *Courage*, mentioned in the previous chapter, is in part a response to the death of his first child, 'who lived only briefly, filled our lives with love, and all too soon left us to aching sorrow'.[12] And it is neither sufficiently appreciated nor understood that political life frequently exacts great personal cost from its practitioners without even the slightest whiff of the aphrodisiac of power by way of compensation:

> Everything you do, at least if you are in national or State politics, will be closely monitored. You will have to work long hours, and be responsive to crises or personal appeals at any time of the day or night. You will have to respond to scores, even hundreds of emails and letters every week, some of them about complicated matters that cannot be answered routinely, some of them highly offensive. Most weekends you will be in your constituency conducting advice sessions, opening fetes, addressing voluntary organisations and being criticized at local party meetings.[13]

At their best, politicians exercise a high calling – a vocation even – as they respond to the opportunities of service and work for change. And when they do fail or fall from grace and resort to behaviour that dismays or disappoints, their redeeming human qualities and gifts still remain. Here is Shirley Williams, a seasoned and highly respected politician across all the parties, recalling a lecture given by President Clinton at the invitation of the BBC in December 2001:

> It was a wonderful lecture, imaginative, empathetic, visionary. From the material of his own experience and memory, he wove a cloth of gold, a shining vision of a world of peace and prosperity which was attainable by today's leaders from today's global resources. Throughout the lecture I was conscious of the man's love for humanity and I am not being sarcastic. Undisciplined and promiscuous he may be, but there is a massive engine of warmth in the man.[14]

The point is well made: either we succumb to the corrosive cynicism that castigates all politicians as charlatans or we choose instead to wrestle with the imperfectability and possibilities of human nature. The latter will require us to recognize that political action will frequently bear the marks of compromise and least worst choices[15] and that those who govern us reflect the height and depth of the human condition – on the one hand the longing for new horizons and impossible dreams and, on the other, the selfishness and egoism that impose their own brutal convictions on everyone and everything else.

Implied in our choice here is the issue of trust and the extent to which we still feel able to believe the words and promises that constitute the policies and manifestos that will shape so many destinies as this fragile century continues to unfold with much fear and trembling. We stand at an interesting juncture, many of us still wounded by the specious arguments based on non-existent weapons of mass destruction that have turned Iraq into a place of desolation and horror, yet now confronted by a British Prime Minister who has spoken openly about the moral compass provided by his Church of Scotland upbringing and who some years ago quoted the prophet Isaiah 'to undo the heavy burdens and let the oppressed go free' in support of the extraordinary Jubilee 2000 campaign that reduced the debt of the world's poorest countries. To some political commentators it seems very odd that a man who waited 10 years to occupy Number 10 could write a book that says nothing about ideology, manifestos or the path to power but concentrates instead on the choices made by individuals who then devote long periods of their lives to great causes with very little by way of power at their disposal. How interesting and potentially significant that such a senior politician, steeped in the craft of government and arcane economic theory, should have chosen the exercise of moral judgement as his preferred subject. The American theologian and social activist, Jim Wallis, who knows Brown well, sees the book as evidence that 'Christian thinking really is very powerful in him . . . he knows the scripture, he knows what God requires'.[16]

For ourselves it may be that what God requires from us just now is a greater capacity to trust. There is evidence that we are becoming more suspicious, less trusting, no longer inclined to defer to the words of authorities and institutions. Yet without a culture of trustworthiness, the civility and sense of belonging that define our common life are threatened. Without trust things fall apart and we are less inclined to believe in common purposes, shared values, the importance of human relationships and our need of others in order to be ourselves.[17] The nurturing of trust lies in the ordinary acts of every day where we help one another without duress or the prospect of gain. Trust, in part, is a matter of public decency and thinking socially as the means of counterbalancing the anti-social trends that corrode our public life. And in a political culture where householders frequently tell local candidates that they are not going to vote because 'They're all the same. They're just in it for what they can get out of it',[18] trust at the present time calls for a small leap of faith and a preparedness to listen without prejudice to those in power in the hope and expectation that lies form no part of their agenda.

The leap of faith in this instance is neither blind nor naive. It rests on the belief that we inhabit an ambiguous rather than a perfect world where saints and sinners are jumbled together in such a way that good things are always possible and frequently emerge from unlikely places. Augustine argued that, just as the Church on earth is a mixed body with some weeds growing among the wheat, in the same way governments have some wheat growing among the weeds. Humanity is bound together until history is over and there is a final harvest and judgement. In the interim we make a big mistake if we suppose that the world represents a contest between sheer evil and perfect good 'at war with each other in the merry midground of human history'.[19] And we are obliged to be charitable concerning the state of others' souls and the motivation behind their deeds: the ambassadors of God may be far away from Church synods and councils and the legions of Satan may be lurking behind Episcopal thrones. Augustine once travelled 120 miles in old age to meet with a commander of the Roman Empire who was contemplating a monastic life of celibacy, poverty and obedience. Augustine made the arduous journey in order to *dissuade* this leader of armies from relinquishing his earthly power for the call of the cloister. For Augustine, preserving political order amounted to a godly vocation if it protected the Christian peace.[20] And, for myself, I am bound to say that politicians who provide this and future generations with good reasons for living and hoping deserve our respect and trust. They help us to map the kingdom and enable a society to see beyond the ersatz icons of selfishness and greed. They also remind us that in order for dreams to be realized much has to be done that is painstaking and mundane. The formulation and implementation of social policies entail endless hard slog but they also help to shape the lives of entire communities. Applying the great love of God to the concrete situations of our communities necessarily requires social and corporate action and a renewed trust in politics as 'the art of the possible'.

I am in no doubt so many years on from those early 'awakenings' in my life that they have fashioned me towards particular purposes. I joined the Anti-Apartheid Movement. I became a member of Amnesty International and campaigned against the ugly face of fascism that was re-emerging in Britain in the guise of The National Front Movement. During the 1980s the renewed threat of nuclear war, high unemployment and urban poverty became dominant issues for the British nation. I felt proud to be actively working in a church that was responding courageously and

and occasionally
the "art of the
impossible"
— Gordon Duff.

imaginatively to the economic and social issues of the day.[21] I tried hard to study the facts – first to understand what was going on, and secondly to answer the common charge that Christians should not become politically involved. I became Vice Chair of a Housing Association and a Board member of a District Health Authority. In the early 1990s I represented the people of Hull through its Community Health Council, initiated a range of Government-backed community projects across the council estate in my city-centre parish and chaired the Church Urban Fund Committee that gave small grants to local church community projects. Currently, in Southport, I serve with local politicians and business leaders on a Partnership Board that is responsible for the economic regeneration of the town.

I recognize a pattern in all this: the desire to take seriously the public issues and situations that form part of the texture of our lives; the need to think theologically about such events as part of the scriptural mandate to read the signs of the times (Matt. 16.3); and the belief that the State, when it genuinely pursues a vision of justice, peace and the common good, is an instrument of God's kingdom. The things of Caesar (Matt. 22.21) are not intrinsically disordered or corrupt and are no more in need of conversion than the rest of us, *provided* they seek to embody the moral principles and ideals that make for human flourishing.

I need to say (if only for my own conscience!) that at no stage have I ever seen myself slipping into the role of political activist to the detriment of my calling. What I have done and continue to do as a priest spring from the basic convictions that we can neither think about, nor pray to, God in a political vacuum and that if the Church is to be a sign of the kingdom in our midst it must always be ready to engage with or challenge earthly powers. Faith is not only about political engagement, because there are key areas of our human experience where politics has no remit – grief, sorrow, the religious search for meaning, our most intimate relationships, the sickness unto death or the hope of a hereafter – but faith loses some of its vitality if it fails or refuses to see the importance of collective action for the sake of those least able to help themselves (Jas. 2.14–17).

I have come to realize that such a stance will some-times be neither understood nor appreciated, both within the Church and beyond. From time to time I have sat in canteens, in boardrooms or housing projects and the inevitable question has been raised concern-ing why I am involved in work that is not obviously religious or church-based. In the 1980s some members of my congregation felt it necessary to attend public meetings I was addressing on the grounds that my bishop would be written to if I appeared to be overly-critical of the Thatcher government. More worryingly, I recall with great clarity the decision to earmark a chapel collection during my ministerial training for the work of the Anti-Nazi League – actively involved at the time in countering the politics and propaganda of the National Front. The collection proved much smaller than usual (a very significant fact) and in due course the College Bursar, enraged by the proposal, refused to send the cheque. A special debate was held in the weekly College Meeting of students and staff and after a vote the money went to the ANL. A small but important victory was gained and a serious argument won. But I learned much more about the

The Bursar said :
" I fought against the
Nazis for 6 years !'

Many
debates of this kind
at dcB!

innate caution that Christians often feel when faith
becomes messy or controversial and strays into political conflict. In this respect it seemed and still seems
that we sometimes fail or refuse to see that the birth,
life and death of Christ carry with them huge social
implications. A crucified Lord, we should remember,
was put to death by the ruling powers and crucified
between two thieves, not two candlesticks. And the
infant born at Bethlehem was quickly exposed to the
wrath of King Herod and the political machinations
of his court. In a short lifetime and an even shorter
and tumultuous ministry, Jesus comforted many
but he also disturbed the social order. We have no
difficulty with the Christ the healer, but the Christ
who casts the money-changers out of the Temple with
barely concealed rage (Jn. 2.13–17) seems to have a
more tenuous claim on our imagination and natural
inclinations.

A final lesson worth sharing here concerns motivation and hope. In working for the kingdom, in trying
to map the gains and losses that enable us, to some
extent, to see evidence of its coming and realization
in such a complex world, what has been, and what
remains my expectation concerning that blessed time
when God's righteousness and truth will cover the
earth ? All those years ago (and remember I am a
peace and love child of the 1960s!) I was less conscious
of the intractability of the world, the workings of the
human heart and just how easily apparent triumphs
and achievements can be undone. The kingdom was
not exactly around the corner but with enough prayer
and perspiration a new world was coming. The
passion remains: I still believe in the possibility of
transformative projects; I desire that the needy should
not be forgotten and that the hope of the poor should

not perish (Ps. 9.18); and I continue to work and pray that the world may be a safer and better place. The language of prayer and the vision of the kingdom remain for me inseparable. They represent my ideals[22] and they enable me to see the imperfections of these fragmented times. And if now they remind me that the fulfilment of such dreams lies beyond my own earthly span or even the best endeavours of humankind (lie, that is, within the gracious realm of the eternal)[23] they still persuade me that I must continue to do the right thing. The love of Christ and the lure of his commands demand no less.

7

The Art of Dying

For those moments in life when as, Wordsworth observed, 'the world is too much with us'[1] the internet now affords us a resting place. By clicking on www. poeticexpressions.co.uk troubled minds can access soothing words that lift and encourage. The poetry speaks to deep but common human predicaments and provides consolation by reminding the reader that many others have found themselves in identical situations before. In relation to death and grief, the most visited reading is 'Death is nothing at all' by Canon Henry Scott Holland. This comes as no surprise to me. The words are frequently to be found on funeral service sheets and are often requested at thanksgiving services for loved ones:

> Death is nothing at all.
> I have only slipped away into the next room.
> I am I and you are you.
> Whatever we were to each other,
> that we are still.
> Call me by my old familiar name.
> Speak to me in the easy way you always used.
> Put no difference into your tone.
> Wear no forced air of solemnity or sorrow.
> Laugh as we always laughed
> at the little jokes we always enjoyed together.
> Play, smile, think of me, pray for me.

> Let my name be ever the household word that
>   it always was.
> Let it be spoken without effect,
> without the ghost of a shadow in it.
> Life means all that it ever meant.
> It is the same as it ever was.
> There is absolute unbroken continuity.
> What is death but a negligible accident?
> Why should I be out of mind
> because I am out of sight?
> I am waiting for you for an interval,
> somewhere very near
> just around the corner.
> All is well.

It is not difficult to account for its appeal. The words are rich with the promise that all shall be well and that death is a temporary inconvenience. Nothing has been lost irretrievably and the presence that we most desire to feel is closer than we can imagine. The way things were remains unbroken. I am asked about this reading so often when death comes home that it would be churlish of me to be unduly critical. It clearly helps many families in their hour of grieving and it speaks directly and confidently to the awful human fear that invariably accompanies loss. But I have reservations. They have nothing to do with the Freudian critique of religion that interprets the consolation of a hereafter as nothing more than metaphysical Smarties for those who cannot face death with a clear eye and prefer a spurious comfort to unvarnished truth.[2] Freud claims too much here and seems unaware of the record of Scripture, which suggests that the religious impulse amounts to far more than 'the projection of our own wishes on to the sky'[3] and is better understood as an exploration of how death can be accepted unflinch-

ingly on its own terms.[4] And I have the greatest respect
and admiration for the eminent Victorian clerical
gentleman who first penned these words to which so
many turn. Henry Scott Holland was a realist who
never evaded hard facts. He inspired his readers to
work for positive change in society, particularly when
dismal economic forces denied the poorest people
health and opportunity.[5] He was also a notable
preacher and 'Death is nothing at all' is, in fact, part
of a sermon preached by him in St Paul's Cathedral
on Whit Sunday 1910, as the body of King Edward
VII was lying in state at Westminster.

The difficulties I have amount to this: it is simply
untrue to assert or believe that death is a relatively
inconsequential fact. All of us know something of
the anxiety and dread that can arise when we are
required to contemplate the end of everything we are
or might still hope to be. The philosopher, Francis
Bacon, expressed this experience succinctly: 'Men
fear death as children fear to go into the dark.'[6]

The fear is universal. It crosses frontiers and
boundaries and individuals of high estate or low are
disturbed by the thought of their own end. London
is bustling at the moment with thousands of visitors
making their way to the central Reading Room of
the British Museum where eight life-size terracotta
warriors stand on a platform in an eerie light. Behind
a pair of generals stand two archers, then a couple of
infantrymen followed by a cavalryman and his horse.
A charioteer brings up the rear. They represent a tiny
part of the buried terracotta army of 7,000 soldiers
that has stood to attention near the city of Xi'an in
China for more than 2,000 years. The head of the
first of them was unearthed in 1974 and excavation

at the site still continues. They were created at the command of the first emperor Ying Zheng, who was born in 259 BC and became Qin at 13. He grew to be a military genius but the domination of neighbouring states did not assuage his more fundamental ambition to be the first to live for ever. He drank various potions to secure this outcome but as a precaution engaged 700,000 men to build his tomb and a surrounding necropolis. Life beyond death was interpreted as a microcosm of life on earth. Qin intended that he would still reign over this unending world and the Terracotta Army would keep eternal vigil to protect it. His soldiers live on as testimony to his ingenuity and ambition and his even deeper desire to escape the eternal cycle of birth, growth, decline and death.

The unease I feel with the notion that death is a trifling thing that should neither mar our enjoyment of life nor distress us overmuch has also to do with the fact that such a claim is bad theology. It goes against the grain of Scripture. Within early Judaism nothing of any worth survived death – what *could* survive it, we may ask, when Adam was fashioned from the dust of the earth? The days of man 'are like a passing shadow' (Ps. 144.4) and the psalmist laments that in death there is no real remembrance of God, only, at best, the shadowy abode of Sheol where memory and hope have no purchase (Ps. 6.4). No one returns from the grave and 'hereafter we shall be as though we had never been' (Wisdom of Solomon 2.2). We can sense a brave, even chilling realism in such passages, and the knowledge that later Judaism came to a view that what is taken back by God at death is neither lost nor destroyed in no way diminishes the strength of the earlier conviction of Israel that the reality of death is to be feared. St Paul speaks in a similar vein in

the New Testament when, with characteristic direct-
ness, he declares that death is 'the last enemy to be
destroyed' (1 Cor. 15.26). An enemy, by definition,
is neither friend nor consoler and comes bearing
threats not gifts. And it is certainly the case that for
Mark, the earliest gospel writer, the death of Jesus
is a horrid thing – an innocent man expiring slowly
on the gallows with words of desperation on his lips:
'My God, my God, why have you forsaken me?' (Mk.
15.34) represents the culmination of the harrowing
process begun in the Garden of Gethsemane when
Jesus clearly did not wish to die (Mk. 14.34–36). The
cup of suffering did not pass from him, but he desired
that it should. It is also significant that when Canon
Scott Holland preached in 1910 following the death
of Edward VII, his sermon was entitled 'The King of
Terrors'. Popular imagination and human need have
now latched on to a particular part of a sermon that,
read in its entirety, does not flinch from the uncom-
fortable fact that death comes to us all.

For the remainder of this chapter I need to address
this central fact – not from a questionable desire to be
needlessly morbid but in the realization that part of
the business of a durable faith is to contend with the
realities we find most hard to bear. Ultimately there
is no hiding place even in the vastness of the world
to shield us from the unease that attends the sure
knowledge that we are perishable clay, that our life
is always slipping away and will, one day, end. The
challenge, surely, is how we learn to live with such
truths in a way that releases us from crippling fear
and enables us to celebrate each returning day.

I shall say more about this later. Before then some
clarifications are required. I am not suggesting that
death is the worst thing that can befall us and as such

requires a category all of its own. There are many human experiences that surpass it in terms of dread, not least, the routine horror of existence that sometimes leads people to embrace suicide in preference to the hollowness or pain of an existence that has become unbearable. As a priest I also know that death is often welcomed when it represents a form of healing or the final fruit of long, productive years. During the past week I have been called on several occasions to the bedsides of the dying: in each case there has been a recognition of who I am, an absence of fear and an acceptance that the road about to be taken is both unfamiliar and inevitable. Such moments can be filled with grace and hope as well as resignation. For many years I have enjoyed and used the poetry of Stevie Smith, an eccentric and engaging woman who came to wide recognition during the last decade of her life as part of the poetry boom of the 1960s. She had strong opinions on many things, wrote with elegance and simplicity on the complex business of living and dying and throughout her life displayed a welcoming attitude to death that astonished her visitors and friends. Shortly before she died in 1971, she sat up cross-legged on her hospital bed and recited her poem 'Come, Death' without hesitation or mistake:

> I feel ill. What can the matter be?
> I'd ask God to have pity on me,
> But I turn to the one I know, and say:
> Come, Death, and carry me away.
>
> Ah me, sweet Death, you are the only god
> Who comes as a servant when he is called,
>   you know,
> Listen then to this sound I make, it is sharp,
> Come, Death, do not be slow.[7]

The importance of the poem lies in its conviction that death can be a liberator – the servant who finally sets us free and brings with it a trembling hope of transformation. Stevie Smith practised the art of dying for the greater part of her life and I suspect this is what enabled her to meet her end with equanimity. Long before she reached the point where her physical powers began to fail she confronted what others choose to ignore or repress – the certainty that death would come to her. This realization was, for her, 'a fortifying thought, good enough to carry me to a ripe old age'.[8] As a controversial agnostic who nevertheless yearned for the love of God she bound herself to the perishable hours of life but was never afraid to let them go.

Her attitude, combined with the integrity of her writing, seems to me to set a gold standard in relation to a deeply sensitive area of human experience that we often shun until it is too late. For understandable reasons most of us have no particular will to dwell on the fact of our mortality, especially at a time when death is banned from polite conversations or shunted off to hospital wards. The persuasive apparatus of advertising and marketing also instil in us the silly notions that we can look young and beautiful for ever 'because we are worth it'. Many seem happy, desperate even, to buy into the illusion, added to which we lack the experts who, like Stevie Smith, can encourage us to dwell a little more on how we might use our days well in the awareness that they are not as numberless as the grains of sand upon the shore. Because we neither seek nor receive instruction, it is easy to remain in a state of permanent denial concerning the one certain fact of our life. When we are young, of course we feel ourselves to be immortal: death is an abstraction and it seems inconceivable that we shall eventually decline and die. The eighteenth-century English essayist William Hazlitt puts it rather well:

> No young man believes he shall ever die . . .
> There is a feeling of eternity in youth which
> makes amends for everything. To be young
> is to be as one of the immortal Gods . . .
> Death, old age, are words without a mean-
> ing that pass by us like the idle air which we
> regard not. As in setting out on a delightful
> journey we strain our eager gaze forward
> and see no end to the landscape.[9]

Even as we advance in years, however, it is still possible to sustain the illusion of immortality. There is much to see and do by way of helpful distractions and as busy people we keep an optimistic eye on a future that will bring us deserved blessings. Philip Larkin's poem 'Next, Please' takes issue with such presumptuous expectations:

> Always too eager for the future, we
> Pick up bad habits of expectancy.
> Something is always approaching; every day
> *Till then* we say.

> Watching from a bluff, the tiny, clear
> Sparkling armada of promises draw near.
> How slow they are! And how much time
> they waste
> Refusing to make haste!

> We think each one will heave to and unload
> All good into our lives, all we are owed
> For waiting so devoutly and so long.
> But we are wrong.

Only one ship is seeking us, a black-
Sailed unfamiliar, towing at her back
A huge and birdless silence. In her wake
No waters breed or break.[10]

Rather like Stevie Smith, Larkin could be difficult,
opinionated and solitary. In relation to death, however, a great chasm divides them. Larkin had a strong
melancholy streak and from a relatively early age
was much preoccupied by the fearful prospect of his
death. 'Next, Please' was written in 1951 when he
was in his late twenties. I first came across it about
the same age and have always been drawn (sometimes
against my wishes!) to its verses and the intimidating
image that concludes the poem – the 'black-sailed
unfamiliar' ship. Here Larkin taps into our deepest
and most private fears but does so in a way that challenges us to deal with them. His daunting gift lies in
his truthfulness concerning what we generally prefer
not to think about. Almost 25 years later he was still a
haunted man, sitting in the quietness of his bedroom
before daybreak, staring at the curtains, waiting for
the light but:

Till then I see what's always there:
Unresting death, a whole day nearer now,
Making all thought impossible but how
And where and when I shall myself die.[11]

To some extent Larkin was crippled by the fierce
contradictions of his nature and the morbidity sometimes verging on self-loathing that cast the deepest
shadows over his days. He could be witty and amus-
ing – he was a great mimic – and he retained a passion
for music, especially jazz. Invited to choose his selection of records on the Radio 4 programme *Desert
Island Discs* he selected four jazz pieces and also a

Thomas Tallis motet, the 'Coventry Carol', Elgar's Symphony Number 1 and Handel's 'Praise the Lord'. An interesting choice given that his agnosticism had never allowed him entry into the Christian fold. At the memorial service held in Westminster Abbey following his death in 1985, more jazz was played. But as the service ended a trumpeter ascended into the organ loft and the sound of 'A closer walk with thee' filled the abbey as the large congregation prepared to leave. There is a touching irony in this closing piece: perhaps somewhere in Larkin's tormented life there was just the slightest glimmer of what Browning had referred to in the previous century as 'the grand Perhaps' – the sense that there could be moments of deep meaning that somehow compensated for, or even transcended, the tragic dimensions of living and dying. Larkin's poetry rarely, if ever, permits such possibilities. Unlike Stevie Smith, who managed the art of portraying death as both merciful oblivion and friend, he saw it instead as 'something one is always afraid of'.[12] In regretting the lopsidedness of his life that kept a good deal of its savour at arm's length and made him neurotically preoccupied with his end rather than the pleasures and duties of the interim, I nevertheless value his writings immensely. In a way perhaps that he neither expected nor necessarily even intended, his poems sometimes carry the reader into the realm of longing, of fresh beginnings and the irrepressible power of hope that fuels our lives and permeates the natural world. Thrilled by the visible renewal of nature he writes:

> Yet still the unresting castles thresh
> In full grown thickness every May.
> Last year is dead they seem to say,
> Begin afresh, afresh, afresh.[13]

If his darker work turns our minds to final ends, and to our own in particular, I am thankful for this too. At the beginning of each Lent as ash is placed upon our foreheads we hear the words 'Remember that dust thou art and to dust thou shalt return.' We are informed in the most direct manner imaginable that we are terminally ill, however short or long we have lived. In their different ways, the poets and Christian liturgy point to the way things are and remind us that concerning such matters we should not be deceived.

Quite possibly you have had enough of this chapter by now and want to put the book down or even throw it with maximum force in the direction of the nearest Oxfam shop! I hope, however, that this is not the case: I am trying to be honest here with a difficult fact that has enormous power to shape our hopes and fears. And I am arguing that unless we begin, in however small a measure, to practise the art of dying we remain unfree, constrained by anxieties that dare not speak their name and fettered by fears that will not let us go because we have consistently refused to recognize them. Only in the steady contemplation of our own mortality can we begin to say 'yes' to the fact that we shall die one day. And only in the benign acceptance of death do we start to remove its sting and terror and live out our destinies as sons and daughters of God. From time to time, following a big funeral or a tragic death in the parish, I have been asked by my younger son whether the prospect of my own death and dying perturbs me. I reply that the answer depends on my state of mind on any given day and the manner of my end. Sometimes life is so full and rewarding that it represents a party that I shall be very reluctant to leave. It seems odd and not a little upsetting that everything will still be going on but I shall not be there. On other days there is something attractive in the knowledge of a final repose where the world can no longer hurt us and God's loving purposes find further expression. I have no wish to live long if I cannot live well (and in relation to my sons they think I have already lived a very long time!). Either way, I have long accepted the necessity of preparation in the hope that when my own departing comes I shall not be unduly afraid. I find strength in the goodness of God and the example of his Son. But I also know that the prospect of the grave will not truly represent 'a bed of hope'[14] until I have come to terms with the facts: I am. I shall die. Yet shall I live. It is, I believe, in the readiness to embrace each one of these religious truths and to give each one its proper due that we find our freedom to live and die without fear or dread.

We could at this point move to the more congenial discourse of the next chapter but I am conscious that two important questions remain. Even within the household of faith it might be objected that thinking about our death in this way is rather self-indulgent and detracts us from the far more important business of living. Would it not be better to concentrate on the here and now? And for those who lack any religious convictions, why not just enjoy the passing scene with its delights in preference to the thought of annihilation? The latter is not a new question. Judaism was acutely aware of the challenge a century before Christ and took issue with the creed of the 'ungodly' that favoured the pleasure principle with its invitation to

> enjoy the good things that exist,
> and make use of the creation to the full as
>   in youth.
> Let us take our fill of costly wine and
>   perfumes,

and let no flower of spring pass us by.
Let us crown ourselves with rosebuds
  before they wither.
Let none of us fail to share in our revelry.
  everywhere let us leave signs of enjoyment
because this is our portion and this is our
  lot.

Wisdom of Solomon 2.6–9

I have some sympathy with the first objection. Part of Philip Larkin's failure as a human being was his indolence or refusal to engage with life beyond the confines of his university library and living-room or his personal relationships that sometimes went awry. To be so fixated with death negates the promise of life in its fullness (John 10.10) as a present reality and denies us the possibility of a genuine sympathy with the lives of others that will frequently be more fraught than our own. Too much time with death diminishes the duties of discipleship. But there is still a balance to be struck. What is lacking in the seductive invitation to pleasure as an alternative way of life is any sense that we are more than creatures of desire. We actually know ourselves to be more than just a bundle of appetites. Our genetic code links us with the higher animals but unlike them we experience the pressure of conscience, the ache of beauty and the intimations of mortality. There is also our thirst for knowledge, the need to understand, and the awareness that we are inextricably caught up in the web of time. Becoming a proper person requires us to think hard about our own natures and how we can function at our best given the kind of creatures we decidedly are.

The fact is, we think and feel in ways that animals denied the gift of language cannot. This does not make us angels, still less God, but as complicated creatures occupying a perplexing place somewhere between earth and sky – the philosopher Pascal describes us in terms of 'the glory and refuse of the earth'[15] – we are obliged, by virtue of our natures (as well as the prompting of our religion) to recognize the provisionality of our lives and bring death occasionally to mind. Once we are able to do this with some consistency, there is a gain. We cease to fret about what is in the long run inconsequential and we may find it easier to forgive our enemies and mend broken relationships. It is 'partly the illusion that we will live forever which prevents us from doing these things'.[16] Becoming properly human, therefore, in relation to our death – giving it some attention before we are ultimately required to do so – makes it less daunting. If not yet a friend, it can cease to be an enemy and instil in us something of how we ought to live. The refusal to acknowledge death paradoxically diminishes our sense of well-being, for we know deep down that its evasion amounts to living a subtle lie. Put in religious terms it also represents a form of 'bad faith', a regrettable disservice to the One who urged us to live in the present moment (Matt. 6.34) but also made his final journey to Jerusalem in the certain knowledge of his own impending end. To believe that notions such as a 'good death' and 'dying well' remain important for the religious life requires that we not only face death with fortitude and hope when it comes but also do our homework beforehand. It is, in the end, an art.

8

The Grace of Words

I am fairly clear that my love of reading goes back to my childhood. By reading I mean not only books but newspapers, journals, comics, the label on the HP sauce bottle that used to be printed in English and French, graffiti on grubby walls, the back or front covers of magazines held by other travellers on the tube or train, the billboards and neon signs of the city and countless Gideon Bibles tucked away in hotel rooms. This long opening sentence represents the confession of a book lover, or a 'bibliophile' according to the dictionary, and I am happy to stand accused. I am not quite in the league of the writer Cervantes who, in his obsession with reading, could not apparently resist even bits of torn paper in the street[1] but my passion for the printed word occasionally leads my wife to doubt my sanity. She will tell you of her incredulity when, after yet another long day, she witnesses the poignant or pathetic sight (depending on your point of view) of her husband still struggling to stay awake in bed after midnight until a tantalizing page or final chapter has been read. In my defence I can go on to plead with some justification that writing or teaching deadlines are looming and there is the moral obligation of decent preparation. But in truth I am a hopeless case, a lost cause, a wounded soul pierced by the mere sound of words and finding endless pleasure in their configurations. In this respect I am heartened by the knowledge that a Hebrew text written around the sixth century – the *Sefer Yezirah* – records that God created the world by means of 32 paths of secret wisdom, 10 *Sefirot* or numbers, and 22 letters.[2] From the *Sefirot* came all abstract things; from the 22 letters were created all the real entities within the three-fold dimensions of the cosmos – the world, time and the human body. This mystical tradition within Judaism invites us to think of the universe as a written book made from numbers and letters. The key to understanding the cosmos depends upon our ability or desire to read these correctly and master their combination. In so doing we learn to give life to a tiny part of that stupendous and colossal text and thereby imitate the Creator. Honesty requires the admission that such extraordinary thoughts do not detain me every day but they do reassure me that books can be magic carpets and reading can draw us to the holy ground that illuminates the world.

When I think about my childhood, I remain surprised that reading took hold of me in the way it did. I grew up in the 1950s in a Britain still cloaked in post-war austerity. Longsight was a predominantly working-class area of Manchester, gentrified by elegant houses on its periphery and a smattering of professional occupations. A century before, construction workers, engine drivers and warehousemen made up its population along with labourers and printers, butchers and tailors, basket-makers and lamplighters, clerks and servants, merchants and medics.[3] The lamplighters and basket-makers had disappeared by the 1950s but the area retained a pleasing diversity and I loved its streets and roads, its corner shops and its Lowryesque neighbourliness. Books were not a prominent feature of my home and I cannot recollect being read to at bedtime apart from my mother's prayer that 'God should bless everyone and make them good'. There was, however, the keen anticipation of Christmas annuals and the special morning of each week when my comics would be waiting on the doormat. And there was the local library. Over the previous century the people of Longsight enjoyed dancing and sport, cinema-going and drinking. But they also believed in self-improvement and education. The *Manchester City News* reported that on 27 April 1878, a social evening or Conversazione was held at the Longsight Liberal Club when the general public was admitted to a large room where their minds were enriched by 'readings, songs and microscopic objects to inspect'.[4] And in 1890, three local councillors, seeking re-election, promised via their broadsheet that they would provide, along with other essential social amenities such as public baths and wash-houses, 'a Reading Room and a Free Library'.[5]

I have no means of knowing but quite possibly their promise led in time to the outwardly unpretentious but, to me, special building that represented the local library some 15 minutes walk from my home. There I discovered *Just William, Billy Bunter, Jennings* and *Rex Milligan* along with other books and tall tales for growing boys. I relished them all and their central characters became my friends. Although I had an older sister she was away from home for the greater part of my childhood and adolescence due to speech and hearing difficulties. I lived in my imagination quite a lot: an upturned stool in the centre of the living room became a small boat in which I sat to negotiate choppy waters; the carpet underneath the stool was a turbulent sea, the nearby table dry land. I always made it to shore, urged on perhaps by the lure of Treasure Island and Long John Silver awaiting me!

After my 11-plus examinations I was introduced to Shakespeare, poetry and Dickens. My English teachers – Miss Wellborn and Miss Lord, God bless them both! – knew their subject and communicated it well. I responded enthusiastically: poetry was a new world and I began to learn by heart 'The Ballad of Sir Patrick Spense'[6] and his tragic story that ends with his demise in a watery grave. I entered a reading competition organized by the British & Foreign Bible Society. I didn't expect to win. Other entrants seemed taller, brighter, better. They included the head chorister at my local church who seemed to excel in everything that mattered – music, singing, football and dating pretty girls! I was given as my passage John 21.15–22, the moving dialogue between Jesus and Peter where the Master instructs the apostle to 'feed my lambs' and follow him. My name was called, I stood before the judging panel and read aloud the words that have never left me. I won, and walked home in a proud and happy daze. The prize was Bunyan's *The Pilgrim's Progress*. It is still on my study shelves.

My own library has grown over the years and books fill every room of our home. I prune a little from time to time but a steady accumulation continues. The contagion has passed to my sons and a sort of unofficial reading competition exists in the household, based on who has read the most books at any given time in the year. As a general rule I ascertain how many are on their lists and then add one more. It makes my elder son furious but it helps to stem my insecurities that they are ahead in the game! I recognize many of my books by their shape and colour or a detail on the dust-jacket. Their physical presence, especially in the sitting-room and study is reassuring and a source of gratitude and pleasure. I find myself surrounded by a compendium of my life – the Russian, French and German authors, so important in my twenties, and the theologians, philosophers, composers and historians who illuminate my path and bring colour to my teaching. In many of my books I find tangible traces of my past: cinema and theatre tickets, thank you cards, receipts, small photos and scribbled notes. They remind me of times and places, voices and people that might otherwise be forgotten as memories fade and time rushes on. My bedside and study also provide launch pads for the books still waiting to be read. They represent a sort of investment in the future. A Jewish academic colleague in America works on the same principle. His unread book pile is even bigger than mine and he figures that he cannot die until his mini-Everest of literature is mastered!

There is, as you would expect, a special place in my study for Bibles, commentaries and devotional books. These represent for me part of the treasures of the Church, the texts and hymns that contain so much spiritual depth and beauty. I cannot have been more than eight when I heard a young girl called Heather sing 'Consider the lilies of the field how they grow' in the Sunday School choir. I was much too shy to tell her how lovely she was but, more positively, I knew that her words were affecting me. It wasn't just her voice or looks or the simple tune; it was the words themselves, lifted from the Sermon on the Mount (Matt. 6.28) that touched me at a new and unexpected level. I left the Sunday school (along with the fragile dream of singing endless duets with Heather on its stage, hand clasped in hand!) and gave my full allegiance to the local church choir. Over eight years I grew to love the religious imagery evoked by the psalms and the cycle of the Christian year. The annual liturgical drama that began with Advent and culminated in the Feast of the Ascension was to mark me. I became familiar with the majestic and sometimes haunting Sunday Collects – 'Lighten our darkness, we beseech thee, O Lord' – and took to heart the words of Scripture that found their way into hymns and anthems. Even in the quietness of a side chapel with only a few people present, the late evening service of Compline cast a spell. Centuries of Christian praying are compressed into this short work of devotion that helps to explain its timeless appeal. I was not aware of this mystical dimension at the time but I was drawn to the psalms that lie at its heart. They fed my imagination and, in time, my faith. Usually we sang unaccompanied and Cardinal Newman's great hymn 'Lead, kindly Light' impressed itself upon me, particularly the opening verse:

> Lead, kindly Light, amid the encircling
>   gloom,
>   Lead thou me on;
> The night is dark, and I am far from home,
>   Lead thou me on.
> Keep thou my feet; I do not ask to see
> The distant scene; one step enough for me.[7]

About 30 years later I reviewed the newly-published diaries of the writer and broadcaster, Malcolm Muggeridge[8] for a national Catholic newspaper. Muggeridge had intrigued me for many years and reading his book *Jesus Rediscovered* in my early twenties took my life in a new direction. The review led to a meeting with the great man and I made my way to his cottage in Sussex filled with excitement and not a little apprehension, given his reputation as a master of satirical wit and, arguably, the finest journalist of his generation. My anxieties eased as we settled down to lunch with his wife Kitty, surrounded by framed photographs on walls and tables of just about every famous politician and statesman of the twentieth century. After lunch we talked at length and I noticed at one point that my host appeared to be dozing off. 'Don't worry,' said Kitty, 'he often does this nowadays in the afternoon, even when guests are present!' A reassuring remark in the circumstances. Before leaving to catch my train back north I asked him if he would inscribe my copy of his diaries. Having penned his good wishes to me he added: 'May he find his way home even tho' the way is long and we are far from home'. I now find increasingly that when I am asked to pray for people whose needs are very great or whose circumstances appear perilous, I ask simply in the silence that 'they may find their way home'. As I pray, the image of the boy that once was me standing in a chapel singing Compline is never very far away.

I cannot imagine that I shall ever want to stop reading or come to regard words as nothing more than impressions on a page. It is not just the tactile pleasure of books and their civilizing influence on a room or the thread of continuity they give to my life. It has more to do with the fact that reading makes me more alive. I have tried to resist the maxim of Gustave Flaubert that we must 'read in order to live'[9] – a great many things other than books fill my days – but I do see how impoverished existence would be without them. If it is the case that the glory of God is only fully revealed in us when we are most truly alive, my sense is that reading lets in the divine light and melts what is frozen within us.

I think here of Augustine in his *Confessions* recalling a desperate moment in his life, weeping under a fig tree as he recalls past sins and fears for his future. Suddenly, from somewhere nearby he hears a child's voice singing a song whose refrain is *tolle, lege*, 'take up and read'. Augustine runs back and picks up the passage from St Paul that he had left unfinished. In silence he reads the first lines on which his eyes fall, an exhortation to 'put on the Lord Jesus Christ, and make no provision for the flesh' (Rom. 13.14). Overwhelmed he comes to the end of the sentence: the 'light of trust' floods his heart and the 'darkness of doubt' is dispelled.[10]

Augustine represents one of many who at a critical point in their lives have found renewed meaning and illumination in a sacred text. As Martin Luther confronted the power of a medieval Roman Church that had grown flaccid and corrupt at the highest level, it was St Paul again who opened a door in his mind and enabled him to stand 'on the most holy gospel of the glory and grace of God'.[11] Two centuries later at a quarter to nine on the evening of 24 May 1738, John Wesley listened to a reading introducing Paul's Epistle to the Romans. He had entered the meeting in Aldersgate Street, London in a depressed state of mind but as he listened he felt his heart 'strangely warmed': 'I felt I did trust in Christ, Christ alone for salvation; and an assurance was given me that he had taken away my sins, even *mine* and saved *me* from the law of sin and death.'[12] He rose to give testimony to what he regarded as the great moment of his conversion that would lead him to work tirelessly for the moral and spiritual reformation of England and the material needs of 'Christ's poor'. Towards the end of his long life he was still standing in snow-filled streets collecting pennies for the destitute and giving generously of his own income to support their desperate lives. If we fast forward again to the early twentieth century we can observe Karl Barth, its greatest Protestant theologian, writing a massive commentary on a single book. Romans represented for him the most important of the epistles of Paul. Unlike the liberal theologians of his day who were preoccupied with critical questions concerning the historical situation from which Paul wrote, Barth took a different tack. Drawing on the existentialism of Kierkegaard, he insisted that Paul had to be read in a new way. The essential requirement now was for a Christian to be confronted by the theological realities faced by Paul and share his understanding of our situation before God. 'If we rightly understand ourselves, our problems are the problems of Paul; and if we are to be enlightened by the brightness of his answers, those answers must be ours . . . '[13] I am interested here in his use of the word 'brightness' and how once again this image of piercing light is seen to rescue us from presumptuous folly or pride if we will only heed the text. Barth's commentary and early theology 'fell like a bomb on the playground of the theologians'[14] and demonstrated once more how a book can be an incendiary device that ignites the heart and the imagination. Like Augustine, Luther and Wesley before him, Barth found in Paul nothing less than the gracious self-disclosure of God that leads to the forgiveness and new life that is to be found in the historic Christ.

My long-standing admiration for these particular saints and scholars owes something to their tenacity and the boldness of their convictions. But my respect is also bound up with their passion for words. Augustine, as we saw in Chapter 2, read the best that would nourish his thought and memory, in his case, the Bible, Virgil, Cicero and the Neoplatonist philosophers. Words for him represented power and wisdom and Christ was his great teacher. His own writings fill many shelves and amongst them are to be found passages of great beauty. I shared the following extract from the *Confessions* with a group of students just a few days ago. Their enthusiastic reaction encourages me to reproduce it here in full. The important point is to note how Augustine draws us into the text. We identify with him and are challenged to reflect on our own understanding of God and how his truth and beauty are disclosed through creation:

> My love of you, O Lord, is not some vague feeling: it is positive and certain. Your word struck into my heart and from that moment I loved you. Besides this, all about me, heaven and earth and all that they contain proclaim that I should love you, and their message never ceases to sound in the ears of all mankind, so that there is no excuse for any not to love you. But, more than all this, *you will show pity on those whom you pity; you will show mercy where you are merciful*; for if it were not for your mercy, heaven and earth would cry your praises to deaf ears.

> But what do I love when I love my God? Not material beauty or beauty of a temporal order; not the brilliance of earthly light, so welcome to our eyes; not the sweet melody of harmony and song; not the fragrance of

flowers, perfumes, and spices; not manna or honey; not limbs such as the body delights to embrace. It is not these that I love when I love my God. And yet, when I love him, it is true that I love a light of a certain kind, a voice, a perfume, a food, an embrace; but they are of the kind that I love in my inner self, when my soul is bathed in light that is not bound by space; when it listens to sound that never dies away; when it breathes fragrance that is not borne away on the wind; when it tastes food that is never consumed by the eating; when it clings to an embrace from which it is not severed by fulfilment of desire. This is what I love when I love my God.

But what is my God? I put my question to the earth. It answered, 'I am not God' and all things on earth declared the same. I asked the sea and the chasms of the deep and the living things that creep in them, but they answered, 'We are not your God. Seek what is above us.' I spoke to the winds that blow, and the whole air and all that lives in it replied, 'Anaximenes is wrong. I am not God.' I asked the sky, the sun, the moon, and the stars, but they told me, 'Neither are we the God whom you seek.' I spoke to all the things that are about me, all that can be admitted by the door of the senses, and I said, 'Since you are not my God, tell me about him. Tell me something of my God.' Clear and loud they answered, 'God is he who made us.' I asked these questions simply by gazing at these things, and their beauty was all the answer they gave.[15]

There is a poet at work here as well as a philosopher and theologian, who touches and tantalizes us with his disarming request that we should give serious thought concerning *precisely what* we presume to love when we speak of our devotion to God. Augustine's question set minds racing in my recent evening class; perhaps it will do the same for you?

Luther was also a devotee of Augustine before he rediscovered St Paul and began writing the biblical commentaries, translations and liturgies that gave a new religious voice and sensibility to the German nation. It seems strange, even amazing, to me now to recall that it was a translation of Luther's preface to the Romans that lifted Wesley from the depths of despondency on that momentous evening in 1738 that led to a new religious movement. Methodism would be grounded in the hymn singing and fellowship of local congregations aided by the organization, preaching and teaching of this extraordinary evangelist who, in addition to writing endless books, also kept a journal over 55 years that ran to a million words. For all his insistence that salvation was by faith alone, Wesley believed in the life of the mind and had high expectations of future ministers. At Kingswood School close to Bristol, he set out a curriculum that would have done credit to a university department. We can find evidence of Augustine, Origen, Tertullian, Cyprian and Chrysostom. But along with the great theologians of the early centuries there is reference to the philosopher Pascal and the poet Spenser's *Faerie Queene*. He even acknowledges Homer's amazing genius, admitting a 'vein of piety' in his work that could edify aspiring preachers.[16]

Students of Barth were also to find in their teacher an engaging combination of classical Christian thinkers and the civilizing texts of European culture. Barth inhabited a 'broad imaginative space'[17] in which his pupils were able to 'witness the dynamics of newly-created thoughts'.[18] Although I resist some of Barth's views and conclusions concerning the nature and task of theology, I warm to his complex personality, his absorption in people, places, ideas and events, and his readiness to read and write extensively concerning the truth he finds not only in 'the strange new world of the Bible'[19] but also in the thought of Kierkegaard, Kant, Dostoyevsky[20] and the sublime genius of Mozart.

Dostoyevsky became my travelling companion when I took a very long train journey to Scotland and back during my career as a personnel manager in the early 1970s. What I remember about that journey now amounts to its purpose – interviewing prospective candidates for a sales vacancy – the fact that I left a new cardigan in the hotel room and it never came back to me, and the much more satisfying thought that British Rail enabled me to read most of Dostoyevsky's *The Idiot* in two extended sittings! His other great novels were soon sought out.

Some sort of dam burst in me about that time or, to extend an earlier metaphor, the ice in my head melted. There was a kind of explosion and hitherto unimagined worlds of depth and meaning emerged before my eyes in the novels of Thomas Mann, Herman Hesse, Albert Camus, Emile Zola, Tolstoy and Solzenhitsyn. Nearer home Thomas Hardy and D.H. Lawrence exerted the same magic. I know precisely where I was when I read some of these books, what I was doing when their opening pages impacted on me and how I reacted. In one instance I am sitting in a café in Birmingham; I have read only one or two pages of

Camus' *The Plague* but already I am lost in another person's mind. Another place: I am relaxing in a suburb of Manchester on a pleasant afternoon but also quite unable to move beyond the first few paragraphs of Lawrence's *The Rainbow*. I feel implicated in the text: in some sense this is *my* story, it's about *my* life, the inchoate thoughts bubbling below the surface of *my* mind – and I am looking upwards in amazement. I don't exactly punch the air or shout 'Allelulia' but there is an epiphany of sorts and I can only express a kind of mute gratitude that someone is making sense of my life. I am, in a memorable phrase of the Canadian novelist Margaret Atwood, 'negotiating with the dead'[21] and Lawrence wants me to know about the mysterious passage of time, the rise and fall of generations and the sheer physicality of the natural world. He brings me a little closer to the truth and in so doing reorders my mind. There is an enlargement of perception and understanding and I know myself better. Hardy and Zola will soon reveal to me the tragic dimension of things and once again I shall be stopped in my tracks, forget to get off the train at my station or hear myself talking aloud to the author because in speaking to me he is also speaking for me. I feel more real and also ridiculously grateful that the particular arrangement of marks on paper is enabling me to 'catch hold'[22] of things in a different way and create a new sort of communion with the world.

I still feel the same about books today, only now I write and review as well as read. Time contracts and I am aware of subtle changes in how I approach books. I am conscious too of the fact that there are works that I shall perhaps never find the time or inclination to read. *War and Peace* waits for me on the landing table in a bright new edition but will I have to break a

limb in order to read it? And will Tolstoy, to say nothing of the Most High God, forgive me if I enter the
portals of heaven with his masterpiece still neglected?
Such questions aside, reading remains a pleasure
and necessity, a duty and delight. Words continue
to sustain me and they feed my faith. This curious
metaphor that encourages us to see books as things
to be tasted, swallowed or digested has its origins in
Scripture. On 31 July 593 BC, by the river Chebar
in the land of the Chaldeans, Ezekiel the priest and
prophet had a vision of fire in which he received a
mandate from the Lord:

> Open your mouth and eat what I give you. I
> looked, and a hand was stretched out to me,
> and a written scroll was in it . . . He said to
> me, Mortal, eat this scroll that I give you
> and fill your stomach with it. Then I ate it;
> and in my mouth it was as sweet as honey.
> (Ezek. 2.8–9, 3.2–3).

Some seven centuries later, St John, recording his
apocalyptic vision on Patmos, received the same revelation as Ezekiel. Awe-struck, he encounters an angel
with an open book and a voice of thunder instructs
him to take the book from the angel's hand:

> So I went to the angel and told him to give
> me the little scroll; and he said to me, 'Take
> it, and eat; it will be bitter to your stomach,
> but sweet as honey in your mouth.' So I took
> the little scroll and ate it; it was as sweet as
> honey in my mouth, but when I had eaten it,
> my stomach was made bitter.

> (Rev. 10.9–10)

If I allow my imagination and memory to brood over these texts, I can see other images, less fabulous in their contrivance but no less powerful. They bring to mind a certain kind of community: the fraternity of readers everywhere who have tasted words and found in them a source of grace. From my reading of Augustine I know that he visited St Ambrose, the fearless and compelling fifth-century bishop of Milan. Augustine had difficulty engaging him in questions, for when Ambrose was not dining frugally or tending the needs of his guests he was alone in his cell with his books. He always read silently, often unaware of the arrival of visitors 'as his eyes scanned the page and his heart sought out the meaning'.[23] If I stay with the image of the cell, I can visualize in a quite different context the frail but strong figure of Aung San Suu Kyi, the brave Burmese resistance leader who has been under house arrest for the past 12 years. For some time she has been denied the opportunity to play the piano in her confinement, an activity that brought her comfort and gave hope to her many followers as they stood outside her house and listened. To hear the piano was to know that she was still alive. It is a text that sustains her, however, even when the music recedes. She meditates frequently upon her Buddhist scriptures and is fed. I have in mind, last of all, the author of the Christian classic that in time became my Bible-reading prize so many years ago. Following his arrest in 1660 for defying the authorities by holding a preaching meeting, John Bunyan spent long years in prison. Out of his silence and solitude came the narrative of the religious life that has exercised such a hold on the imagination of its readers. *The Pilgrim's Progress* (1678) is Bunyan's book but it is our story. Its author bids us embark on a journey where there will be 'light and darkness, mountain and valley, tranquillity and torment'.[24] But his book will be sufficient to guide and feed us as we go:

> This book will make a Traveller of thee;
> If by its counsels thou wilt ruled be;
> It will direct thee to the Holy Land,
> If thou wilt its directions understand.[25]

The first requirement on our part is to take up the book and read. The words stand eager and attentive, waiting to take us home.

9

On Being Good

The story of my visit to Malcolm Muggeridge in the previous chapter prompted me to dip into his diaries again. One of the first entries I came across is dated 5 January 1954. It begins:

> Bad night full of dark fears. While shaving suddenly thought with infinite longing how, of all things, I'd most love to live a Christian life. This is the only wish now, I'd ever have. And yet other satisfactions, known to be spurious, still pursued.[1]

The entry would have surprised the obituary columnists when they marked his death in 1990. Most of them praised his skills as a journalist and broadcaster but some questioned the genuineness of his conversion to Christianity, interpreting it as a bogus consolation of his old age after a lifetime of pleasure during which he frequently mocked the pretensions of religious institutions. The historian A.J.P. Taylor was nearer the truth in his appreciation of an old friend. Replying to the charge that Muggeridge had been an embittered cynic for much of his life, Taylor wrote:

> Malcolm was a cynic who got great fun out of it . . . The greatest change in him was his discovery of God and Jesus Christ . . . I cannot explain or even describe what hap-

pened to Malcolm. All I know is that he was utterly sincere.[2]

The fascination of the diaries for me has always had to do with their honesty as much as their style and wit. Muggeridge writes candidly of his achievements and affairs, his bewilderment and restlessness, his sporadic sense of futility despite the outward trappings of success and contentment, and his longing to be a better person. For all his indifference to catechisms and creeds, and his mocking of the more vapid utterances of Church leaders, the lure of religion is never very far away. In the pages of the gospels and the epistles of Paul, he sometimes sees a light that will in the end prove irresistible. He honestly desires to lead a good life for what he sees in the mirror pains him. But he is also weak and wise enough to recognize that this will prove a strenuous business. The call of Christ requires that he should be perfect, not slightly improved. In this respect he would have understood very well some recent words by Archbishop Rowan Williams: 'Looking at Jesus seriously changes things; if we do not want to be changed, it is better not to look too hard or too long.'[3]

Muggeridge wanted to change – he had felt a stranger in the world for most of his life – and even in his youth the sight of a cross represented hopes and desires from which he turned away. Like Bunyan's Pilgrim, he hurried on, encountering 'stumblings, wrong turnings and false destinations'[4] until in the 1960s, like so many wayward sojourners before him, he became captive to the person and teaching of Christ. He likens himself to the child who had despaired of ever receiving presents suddenly being shown a Christmas tree loaded with gifts. Old friends shook their heads and others thought he was mad. The tabloids conferred upon him the title of 'St Mugg'. He did not mind and began to write and speak more openly of his conversion. He received thousands of letters from readers (including me) that he placed in a large metal box in the hope that one day, after his death, they would reveal the 'extraordinary spiritual hunger'[5] of the age. And in his own long search he rediscovered a deep love of humanity, seeing Christ in 'an old coloured shoe-shine man on a windy corner in Chicago one February morning, smiling from ear to ear; or a little man with a lame leg in the Immigration Department in New York, whose smiling patience as he listened to one Puerto Rican after another seemed to reach from here to eternity'.[6]

Muggeridge's story mirrors the desire of many people to lead a better life even when confronted with the knowledge that we are all divided selves frequently given to false turns, bad thoughts and backward steps. In relation to a faith that aspires to some real moral integrity we need to ascertain what a genuinely good life might look like and how we make ourselves better. The insights of moral philosophy suggest that the process has to do with the cultivation of goodness and virtue in such a way that when moments of choice arrive (whether simple or complicated) we aim to act rightly.[7] Motivations and desires come into play here and the extent to which we can purify and redirect energies so that our life is 'lived out of God, not out of self'.[8] Muggeridge finds this extremely difficult and he concedes that the diaries contain a 'sorry record' of folly, selfishness and stupidity. His candour is disarming and raises the question of how much truth we are able to muster as we reflect upon the tangled web of our own histories and our dealings with others. Some truth can emerge if we allow ourselves to be confronted with the person of Christ, and then ask ourselves if we approve of what we see when we look in the mirror. Christ has many guises and he is not confined to the pages of the gospels that bear such profound witness to his power. He came to Muggeridge in a shoe-shine man and, conspicuously, through the writings of St Paul, Augustine, Bunyan and Blake, Tolstoy and Dostoevsky, Bonhoeffer and Simone Weil.

Personal relationships were also a source of divine illumination. In the grace and forgiveness of his wife Kitty, he found depths of goodness to which he could only aspire. Through his lifelong friendship with the priest and theologian Alec Vidler – known affectionately in later years as 'The Doctor' – he received a comfort and reassurance that never failed and was experienced by Muggeridge as a gift from heaven.[9] There was also the life-changing meeting with Mother Teresa of Calcutta when he experienced in her house for the dying a luminous love 'like the haloes artists have seen and made visible around the heads of their saints'.[10]

In old age, before the onset of his mental decline, Muggeridge achieved the serenity that had so often eluded him in earlier years. He lived an increasingly abstemious life and joined the Roman Catholic Church. The simple pleasures of friendship, reading and walking filled his days. His dying was less than easy and after receiving the last rites he found his release on 14 November 1990.

In some respects he had always been a morally serious person – his satire and invective was more often than not directed at those aspects of the world that he found ridiculous or absurd and at public figures who were vain, pompous or just second-rate. He was capable of the sort of honesty about others that frequently gets us into trouble and he never deferred to risible reputations. As his biographer Richard Ingrams observed:

> My personal and strongest impression, whether reading him or listening to him face to face, was of a man who told the truth – not as a result of any special scruples or sense of religious obligation, but because he was blessed with natural powers of insight and occasionally of prophecy which enabled him intuitively to see events and people for what they were.[11]

His moral seriousness was not without contradictions, however. He was not always honest with those closest to him and his marital infidelities had brought Kitty to the verge of despair. He lacked the will to act on his better intentions and frequently gave in to his more reckless impulses with bad consequences all round. When moments of moral choice arose he often chose badly and in the aftermath entertained fantasies of running away. None of this is exceptional as human life or the Christian gospel goes. Muggeridge was a prodigal son who squandered his inheritance but finally found his way home. He was a sinner who, in recognizing his need to repent of his sins, also knew that in some mysterious way he was 'ransomed, healed, restored, forgiven'.

We can choose to see his life as a retelling of the 'old old story', the accomplishment of love's work and the persuasiveness of divine grace in the most stubborn and unpromising lives. But there is a deeper wisdom available to us from his personal history that relates to the earlier question concerning what a good person is actually like. When we have made allowance for human frailty, how does a person qualify, so to speak, as a candidate for goodness and what gets in the way?

To tackle these questions we need to stay with Muggeridge a little longer. As I now see him, his lapses constitute not only a failure of the will but also of the *moral imagination*. With regard to the former he knows himself all too well and in his novel, *Affairs of the Heart*, he obliquely acknowledges his tendency to abandon projects and relationships:

> It is always an alluring prospect to drop anything – a job, a love affair: to creep out in the darkness from a play just before the curtain rises. You walk out through those swing doors never to return: you buy a ticket at the guichet and go elsewhere, you shut a door behind you, leaving forever unpaid bills, unanswered letters, uncompleted projects, dead hopes and dead desires. An illusory vista of release presents itself: on each voyage the sailor has the same sense of relief at seeing land disappear from sight but as soon as he can see it no more, he is eagerly scanning the horizon for something to break the empty monotony.[12]

The insight that is so evident here serves him less well when his attention is directed away from the endless complications of his own life to the business of the wider world. If he is often astute and wickedly funny in his depictions of worldly pomp and vanities, he is in other instances just wrong – premature in his judgements, hurtful in his remarks and sometimes unable to see the moral decencies and truths that lie beneath or behind the institutions and individuals he caricatures or rejects. As an 'outsider' he cares little for theology, doctrines, creeds or sacraments and in relation to organized religion he is prone to fixed ideas that are little better than prejudices. In choosing not to belong to the Church or become a practising Christian in communion with others for so much of his life, he misreads the signs, cuts himself off from the structures of grace and fellowship that could brighten his conscience and fails to grasp that beyond his own faltering and highly subjective approach to the religious life there exists a corporate dimension to believing that could foster his desire to lead a better life. Faith comes from hearing (Rom. 10.17) but it is also the fruit of sharing what we hold in common in Christ. Muggeridge bypasses both and opts instead for the rootless individualism – 'the believing without belonging' – that is such a marked feature of contemporary life. The Christian past holds little interest for him or, for that matter, how a worshipping community can shape individual lives to better purposes. In later years he will discover a personal, saving truth in Jesus Christ but so often in the diaries he is unable to see that Christian truth is also communal and arises out of the shared experience of those who gather in the name of God, bear each other's burdens, become Christ for others and encourage one another to reflect more deeply on 'things of good report' (Phil. 4.7).

I blush a little here. Part of Muggeridge's attraction when I first read him in what now seems a previous life had to do with the fact that he reflected my own negative feelings about the Church. I had ceased to attend regularly and the institution (as so often appears to youthful minds) seemed to have lost its way and was far removed from the revolutionary zeal and compassion of the New Testament. Muggeridge articulated and reflected my disappointment and frustration but also enabled me to hold on to what I knew, or hoped, would always remain important in a world too easily swayed by trivialities. Eventually I found my way back. The intervening years have reminded me (often painfully) that the disillusionment I had felt at the time was in some measure justified. I continue to believe, however, that the Church represents Christ's Body, is still capable of a prophetic word and brings together week by week in a remarkable way the hopes and fears of so many people. If it has a claim on our allegiance, or asks that we should encourage others to belong, it can only be on the grounds that it helps us grow as persons, blessed with the sort of moral imagination that stops us from getting other people wrong or hurting them. There can be few congregations that do not have a saint or two tucked away in a corner quietly saying their prayers and redeeming their bit of the world through unheroic acts and the grace of their disposition. Their goodness is contagious. Along with the sacraments and the proclamation of the word it constitutes the true treasure of the Church and helps us to conform our lives more closely to the 'Holiest of Holies, Jesus Christ our Lord'.[13] It also encourages me to remain hopeful and to pray the following words with some integrity and expectation:

> O God of unchangeable power and eternal light, look favourably on thy whole Church, that wonderful and sacred mystery; and by the tranquil operation of thy perpetual providence, carry out the work of man's salvation; and let the whole world feel and

see that things which were cast down are being raised up, that those things which had grown old are being made new, and that all things are returning to perfection through him from whom they took their origin, even through our Lord Jesus Christ.[14]

I am not sure that Muggeridge ever saw the Church as a 'wonderful and sacred mystery' that assists our moral flourishing and strengthens our belief through belonging. His rootlessness stymied his wish to become a good man and curtailed the depth that is essential for the cultivation of a moral life. A powerful case can be made for seeing religion and morality in terms of depth. About the time that Muggeridge was regaining his faith after the wilderness years, his old friend Alec Vidler – 'The Doctor' – was writing a biographical sketch of Friedrich von Hügel,[15] who had come to prominence in the early years of the twentieth century with his major work on the mystical element in religion.[16] Von Hügel was a remarkable individual who made a profound impression on those who met him or heard him speak. After his death in 1925, an obituary in *The Times* read:

Those who heard the Baron speak . . . will never forget it – the grey hair standing up from his forehead, the large dark eyes in a face of fine ivory, the divine fire which seemed to fill him, the persistent sense of the reality of God, which broke forth in volcanic utterance, strange bits of slang and colloquialisms mingling with magnificent phrases, and left him, when he ended, exhausted and trembling.[17]

Another obituary, this time in the *Jewish Chronicle,* was even more personal:

> The feeling deepened with each conversation one had with Baron von Hügel that one was in the presence of a very big man, and a man, moreover, who was peculiar, beautiful and a rare combination of scholar and saint.[18]

Both obituaries are new to me but for some time I have valued von Hügel's insight that religion is the *deepest* form of life. As a Roman Catholic he found immense resources in faith: from its depths came 'heroisms, sanctities, spiritualities' and he thanked God for them. He knew that faith was a great ocean of submerged treasures and that in order to recognize and appropriate them it was necessary to be attentive and still. Muggeridge, by contrast, rarely stood still, and when he did he was like a child on the beach, unaware that there was a great ocean all around him. His attention strayed in the wrong directions and his self-absorption limited his moral imagination. He never thought about consequences, and his diary entries do not suggest that 'he had any real qualms about his actions'.[19]

If he could have stood still a little longer and learned from his friend, Alec Vidler, he might have discovered that the good life is bound up with the prayer that goes beyond asking and is 'simply an attention to God which is a form of love'.[20] Prayer introduces the possibility of grace that is able to overcome our human limitations and redirect our energies and emotions towards the mind of Christ (Phil. 2.2). When the time comes to act well or decently, we shall not be surprised to discover that how we behave or react, and the sort of choices we make, will depend on that which most fundamentally claims our attention and compels our allegiance. Our capacity for goodness then becomes less a matter of keeping commandments or reciting creeds and more an internal disposition, an acquired habit of the heart and a way of looking at God that gets our restless self with its fractious desires off our hands.

The depth that grows out of prayer and makes possible the ideal of goodness is also bound up with silence. These final words are being penned at the beginning of Advent, and in keeping with previous years I am re-reading a book that has become a contemporary classic of the spiritual life, *The Coming of God* by Maria Boulding.[21] As a nun living as a hermit she knows very well the ambivalence we often feel towards God: on the one hand desiring him and, on the other, often so daunted by the struggle of living that we can find neither time nor space to know God's presence. She writes to encourage us:

> Silence is partly our interior quality; you can learn to live from your own deep centre rather than in the ego with its clamorous demands. You can make use of any period of silence that does occur, rather than looking on it as an empty stretch of time to be endured or filled up somehow. Silence like this is not a threat to us but an invitation to depth, to listening, to a loving communion in joy . . . This is what Advent is about, but it is also a general law of our lives which are an Advent. You have to wait in hope, waiting for the mystery to unfold, going on doing ordinary things but all the time listening, pondering, growing and energetic-

ally serving. You have to be silent before the mystery.[22]

If, like Muggeridge, we find ourselves fighting gravity, the downward pull of our human nature, we can through silence also become aware of the love of God that bids us welcome even when we draw back or want to run away. Simone Weil, lauded by Muggeridge in his later years as the most luminous intelligence of the twentieth century, likens faith to a seed that is planted in us by the grace of God. In her most widely read book, *Waiting on God*, she writes that 'God places in us a little seed of faith and goes away. From that moment God has nothing more to do, nor have we except to wait.'[23]

The seed grows in relation to our capacity for depth, our attention to the right things and our readiness to pray. Goodness grows in proportion to the object of our deepest desires, the holy lives we emulate that make God real and our ability to wait. Such truths are as old as Christianity yet there is a frequent need on our part to be reminded of them. By responding to the light that is in us, it encourages us to be better, not slightly improved, and lifts our eyes and hearts to God, the source of all goodness.

The philosopher and writer Iris Murdoch struggled with the idea of goodness, finding it 'both rare and hard to picture'.[24] She thought it was most likely to be found in simple people or lives of humility that were free 'of the anxious and avaricious tentacles of the self'.[25] In so far as we find such lives in the household of faith they will often be the ones who pray and for whom life is always Advent. In their preparedness to wait and be still, they show us what goodness is like and direct us to the great Sun we often fail to see.

Notes

Chapter 1

1. 7 February 1970. Cited in Michael Mayne, *This Sunrise of Wonder*, Fount, 1995, p. 13.
2. Richard Dawkins, *The God Delusion*, Transworld, 2006, Bantam Press.
3. Part of a famous essay 'Possible Worlds' by J.B.S. Haldane. Dawkins, *The God Delusion*, p. 364.
4. The Alister Hardy Research Centre at Oxford has compiled over 5,000 accounts of ordinary people 'who have been conscious of, and perhaps been influenced by, some power, whether they call it the power of God or not' and were prepared to write a simple and brief account of these feelings and their effects. See Mayne, *This Sunrise of Wonder*, p. 34.
5. Rudolf Otto, *The Idea of The Holy*, was first published in 1917 and has proved one of most successful theological works of the twentieth century. It has never been out of print and is now available in about 20 languages.
6. John Updike, *Self-Consciousness*, Penguin, 1990, p. 235.
7. See Randal Keynes, *Annie's Box: Charles Darwin, His Daughter and Human Evolution*, HarperCollins, 2001.
8. Franz Kafka, *Metamorphosis and Other Stories*, Penguin Modern Classics, 2007.
9. See *New Scientist*, 'Mysteries of the Deep', 4 Sept 2006.
10. *City of God*, Book 21, 4. edited by David Knowles, Penguin Pelican, 1972.
11. *City of God*, Book 21, 4.
12. *City of God*, Book 14, 24.
13. *City of God*, Book 21, 7.
14. *City of God*, Book 21, 7.
15. Sara Maitland, *A Big-Enough God*, Mowbray, 1995, p. 63.
16. Prayer of General Thanksgiving, *Common Worship*, Church House Publishing, 2000, p. 109.

141

17. Annie Dillard, *Pilgrim at Tinker Creek*, Jonathan Cape, 1975.
18. Dillard, *Pilgrim at Tinker Creek*, pp. 2–3.
19. Dillard, *Pilgrim at Tinker Creek*, pp. 119,121,124.
20. *The Collected Poems of Edwin Muir 1921–1958*, Oxford University Press.
21. See for e.g. 'The Spacious Firmament on High' in particular v.1. (New English Hymnal No. 267).
22. Emily Bronte, 'Last Lines' in *Best Loved Poems,* edited by Neil Philip, Little, Brown, 2000, pp. 80–81.
23. Bronte 'Last Lines', p. 80.

Chapter 2

1. See www.users.drew.edu.
2. The massive labour was a shared undertaking with his former examiner and later friend and colleague Alfred North Whitehead, who was, by general consent, the clever mathematician. He devised the structure of the book and designed most of its symbols. See Peter Watson, *A Terrible Beauty: A History of the People and Ideas that Shaped the Modern Mind*, Weidenfeld & Nicolson, 2000, p. 101.
3. Volume 1 appeared in 1910.
4. Bertrand Russell, *History of Western Philosophy*, Routledge Classics, 2004.
5. 'It is a natural form of curiosity to be interested in the personalities of leading figures in any field. Philosophy is no exception.' Quotation of Bryan McGee, *Man of Ideas*, BBC, 1798, p. 12.
6. Arthur Schopenhauer (1788–1860). His philosophical masterpiece is *The World as Will and Representation,* published in 1819.
7. Cited in Jeremy Stangroom and James Garvey (eds.), *The Great Philosophers*, Eagle Editions Limited, 2006, p. 92.
8. Ludwig Wittgenstein (1889–1951). His two most important works are *Tractatus Logico-Philosophicus* (1922) and *Philosophical Investigations,* published posthumously in 1951.
9. See 'On Truth and Lies in a Nonmoral Sense', in *Philosophy and Truth: Selections from Nietzsche's Notebooks of the Early 1870s*, ed. and trans. Daniel Breazeale, Atlantic Highlands, N.J.: Humanities Press International, 1979, p. 79.
10. 1 Cor. 13.12.

11. Saint Thomas Aquinas (1225–74) gave rise to the Thomist school of philosophy and proved the central figure in the scholastic tradition.
12. Still incomplete at his death, *Summa theologiae* covers 60 volumes with detailed reflection and argument that continues to be influential in shaping religious and philosophical thinking. For a comprehensive introduction to Aquinas' thought and teaching see Brian Davies, *The Thought of Thomas Aquinas*, Clarendon Press Oxford, 1993.
13. Davies, *The Thought of Thomas Aquinas*, p. 15.
14. Tertullian, Quintus Septimus Florens 160–225. African Church Father brought up as a pagan and converted to Christianity before 197.
15. See Alister McGrath (ed.), *The Christian Theology Reader*, Blackwell, 1995, p. 5.
16. Lewis Carroll, 'Why, sometimes I've believed as many as six impossible things before breakfast.' *Alice in Wonderland*, cited in *The Oxford Dictionary of Quotations*, OUP, 1980, p. 135. See also Lewis Wolpert. *Six Impossible Things Before Breakfast: The Evolutionary Origins of Belief*, Faber & Faber, 2005.
17. Rom. 1.20 provides a scriptural underpinning of this view.
18. Source: *de doctra Christiana*, 11. x1. 60–61; in *Florilegium Patristicum*, vol.29. ed. H.J. Vogels, Bonn: Peter Honstein, 1930, 46, 7–36.
19. Richard T. Hughes, *How Christian Faith can Sustain the Life of the Mind*, Eerdmans 2001, p. 34.
20. Rorty sets out his stall in his two early books, *Philosophy and the Mirror of Nature* (1979) and *Consequences of Pragmatism* (1982).
21. Jane Smiley, *Thirteen Ways of Looking at the Novel*, Faber & Faber, 2005. Cited in review by Diana Athill in *Literary Review*, May 2006.

Chapter 3

1. Walter Whitman, 1819–92. American poet, essayist, journalist and humanist. His most famous work is *Leaves of Grass* which he continued to edit and revise until his death.
2. Dr Samuel Johnson wrote perceptively concerning our need 'to fill the vacancies of attention and lessen the tediousness of time'. See *Rambler* No. 85 in Johnson's *Works*, Oxford, 1825, 2. 402.

3. Andrew Shanks, *Faith in Honesty: The Essential Nature of Theology*, Ashgate, 2005, p. 2.
4. Cited by J. Moltmann, *The Crucified God*, SCM Press, 1974, p. 220.
5. Fyodor Dostoevsky, *The Brothers Karamazov*, Heinemann, 1948, p. 249.
6. The philosopher Søren Kierkegaard, 1813–55, described this ambiguity in terms of our 'double-mindedness'. We profess to desire the Good but all the time we are deflected from this by less worthy and inferior considerations. See his *Purity of Heart is to Will One Thing*, Fontana, 1961.
7. From *The Lutheran Book of Worship*, Augsburg, 1978.
8. Anthony Bridge, *One Man's Advent*, Collins Fount, 1985, p. 150.
9. This is an important principle in theology intended to show that divine grace does not replace human nature but perfects it (originally attributed to Thomas Aquinas).
10. W. Somerset Maugham, *The Summing Up*, Penguin, 1971, pp. 44–45.
11. John Hick, *Faith and Knowledge*, Fontana, 1974, p. 98.
12. Cited by Robert Llewelyn, *With Pity Not With Blame*, Darton, Longman & Todd, 1982, p. 128.
13. Dostoevsky, *The Brothers Karamazov*, p. 249.
14. This basic attitude does not have to be synonymous with a fully developed religious faith. Austin Farrer describes it as 'initial faith . . . that attitude of openness or responsiveness through which we move towards an acknowledgement of God's existence'. See his *Saving Belief*, Hodder & Stoughton, 1967, p. 31.
15. Quotation from article by Rt. Revd. P. Walker, *Church Times*, 24 December 1992.
16. Cited by Timothy Gorringe in *God's Theatre: A Theology of Providence*, SCM Press, 1991, p. xii.

Chapter 4

1. 'Frolic on crested and scallop-edged waves!
   Gorgeous clouds of the sunset!
   Drench with your splendour me,
   Or the men and women generations after me!
   Cross from shore to shore, countless crowds of passengers!
   Stand up, tall masts of Manhattan!
   Stand up, beautiful hills of Brooklyn.

Notes

From 'Crossing Brooklyn Ferry' in David S. Reynolds (ed.), *A Historical Guide to Walt Whitman*, New York, OUP, 2000, pp 187–88.

2. Roland Bainton, *Here I Stand*, Nashville, 1950. For a more up-to-date account of Luther's achievements see Derek Wilson, *Out of the Storm: The Life and Legacy of Martin Luther*, Hutchinson, 2007. See also Diarmaid MacCulloch, *Reformation: Europe's House Divided 1490–1700*, Allen Lane, 2003 for a brilliant and comprehensive account of the impact of the Reformation on religion, politics, society and culture.

3. Andrew Roberts, 'A Date with History' in *Literary Review*, August 2006, p. 1. In support of *History Matters*, Roberts notes:

> We have periodic newspaper reports showing how ignorant many of our country-men are about even the most basic aspects of the past. The fact that only 45 per cent of Britons associate anything at all with the word 'Auschwitz' should shake us all out of any complacency we might have.
>
> In recent surveys nearly three-quarters of 11-18-year-olds did not know that Nelson's flagship at the Battle of Trafalgar was called HMS *Victory*. One in seven adults thought that the Battle of Hastings was a fictional event; nearly a third of teenagers who knew that it did really take place nonetheless thought that Oliver Cromwell fought in it. Fewer than half of 16-to-24-year-olds knew that Sir Francis Drake was involved in the defeat of the Spanish Armada, with 13 per cent thinking it was beaten by Horatio Hornblower. There is an open and widening oubliette in our collective knowledge of the past, which needs to be filled. It can't just be done by historians writing for mature audiences.

4. See 'After Working Queens Streets, It's Bunk Beds, Make-up and Mars', article, *The New York Times*, Section B1, Wednesday 2 May 2007.

5. See for e.g. Isaiah 59.8: 'The way of peace they do not know, and there is no justice in their paths. Their roads they have made crooked; no one who walks in them knows peace.'

6. Ramsay MacMullen, *Voting about God in Early Church Councils*, Yale University Press, 2006.

7. J.N.D. Kelly, *Early Christian Doctrines*, A&C Black, 1977,

5th edition. J.N.D. Kelly, *Early Christian Creeds*, Longman, 1972, 3rd edition.

8. See Rod Garner, *Facing the City: Urban Mission in the 21st Century*, Epworth Press, 2004, pp. 21–23.

9. These councils are: Nicaea (325); Constantinople (381); Ephesus (431); Chalcedon (451); Constantinople II (553). Two other ecumenical councils followed at Constantinople III (680) and Nicaea II (787).

10. Henri de Lubac, *Paradoxes of Faith*, San Francisco, Ignatius Press, 1987, p. 145.

11. MacMullen, *Voting about God*, p. viii.

12. MacMullen, p. 58.

13. MacMullen, p. 64–65.

14. For an important account of the origins of the Shia-Sunni conflict see Vali Nasr, *The Shia Revival: How Conflicts within Islam Will Shape the Future*, Norton & Company, 2007.

15. Rowan Williams, *Why Study the Past? The Quest for the Historical Church*, Darton, Longman & Todd, 2005, p. 28.

16. Rowan Williams, *Why Study the Past?*, p. 3.

17. Taken from John Henry Newman, *Idea of a University*, and cited by Robert Van de Weyer and Pat Saunders in *I Step, I Mount: The Vision of John Henry Newman*, Marshall Morgan and Scott, Lamp Press, 1989, p. 73.

18. *Confessions*, V11. 10.

19. 'My dear friend, clear your mind of cant; you may talk in this manner; it is the mode of talking in society; but don't *think* foolishly.' Quotation of Dr Samuel Johnson cited in Ben Wilson, *Decency and Disorder: The Age of Cant 1789–1837*, Faber & Faber, 2007.

20. See 'Afternoon Service at Mellstock (circa 1850)' in Norman Page (ed.), *Thomas Hardy: Everyman's Poetry*, J.M. Dent, Everyman, 1998, pp. 63–64.

21. See Claire Tomalin, *Thomas Hardy: The Time Torn Man*, Penguin Viking, 2006, p. 78.

22. Part of a diary entry by Elliott Felkin, a young army officer, following a visit to the Hardys between Oct. 1918 and Aug. 1919. Recorded in *Encounter*, 18 April 1962, pp. 27–33.

23. In 1924 he publicly attacked the Dean of Westminster for refusing to allow a memorial to Byron in Poets' Corner. 'Whatever Byron's bad qualities, he was a poet and a hater of cant.' Part of a letter to Sir Rennel Rodd, 27 June 1924, *Letters*, V1. 262.

24. Rowan Williams, *Why Study the Past?*, p. 102.

25. Claire Tomalin, *Thomas Hardy,* p. 379.
26. The American literary critic Harold Bloom has recently produced a fascinating study of the various – and even contrary – forms of wisdom that have shaped our thinking. See his *Where Shall Wisdom Be Found?*, Ravenhead Books, 2004.
27. A classic example of this genre is Edward Gibbon's remarkable *The History of The Decline and Fall of the Roman Empire* first published between 1776 and 1778. Alongside the close attention to detail and the wit, Gibbon relishes the opportunity to use irony and a very understated cynicism in his account of the emergence of Christianity and its eventual adoption as the religion of the Roman Empire. See Edward Gibbon, *The Decline and Fall of the Roman Empire,* edited and annotated by Anthony Lentin and Ben Norman, BCA Wordsworth Edition Ltd, 1998, ppxiii–xiv.
28. See 'Christianity reborn', article in *The Economist,* 23 December 2006, p. 84.
29. Albert Camus, *The Plague,* Penguin Modern Classics, 1977, p. 252. In a speech given in 2004 Pope Benedict XVI said 'There exist pathologies in religion that are extremely dangerous and that make it necessary to see the divine light of reason as a controlling organ.' From article 'Keeping the Faith' in *The New York Times Magazine,* 8 April 2007, pp. 40–41.
30. John Henry Newman, *On Consulting the Faithful In Matters of Doctrine,* ed. John Coulson, Collins Flame Classics, 1986, p. 77.
31. Newman, *On Consulting The Faithful,* p. 76.
32. Newman, *On Consulting The Faithful,* p. 76. In this respect it is significant how little attention has been paid to the voice of the laity in the continuing debate over gay clergy within the Anglican Communion – an acrimonious and deeply divisive debate fuelled largely by opposing bishops, theologians and clergy. History repeats itself!
33. Cited by Dom Gregory Dix in *The Shape of The Liturgy,* Dacre Press, A&C Black, 1945, p. 745.
34. Austin Farrer, *The End of Man,* SPCK, 1973, p. 157.

Chapter 5

1. Christopher Meyer, *D.C. Confidential* cited in part of 'Faith and the Future of the Earth', St George's Windsor Lecture

given by James Jones Bishop of Liverpool, 1 June 2007,
p. 2.

2. *The Truth Seeking Heart: Austin Farrer and His Writings,*
edited and introduced by Ann Loades and Robert MacSwain,
Canterbury Press, 2006.
3. Principally Matthew, Mark and Luke. The Gospel of John is
a late work and refers only once to the kingdom expressly.
4. In this respect, the concluding section of his letter to the
Romans is seen by many scholars as a primer in Christian
ethics. See Chapters 12–15.
5. His letter to the Galatians has the single purpose of setting
down true religion against its detractors.
6. See for e.g. E.P. Sanders, *Paul, the Law and the Jewish People,*
SCM Press, 1985.
7. *The Truth Seeking Heart,* p. 28.
8. *William Blake,* selected and edited by Peter Butter, Everyman
Paperbacks, 1996, p. 68.
9. See Alan Ecclestone, *A Staircase for Silence,* Darton, Longman and Todd, 1977, p. 37.
10. I came across this description in a 1976 book on St Paul by
Michael Grant.
11. 1 Thess. 5.17.
12. See J.L. Houlden, *Paul's Letters from Prison,* SCM Press,
1977.
13. See Bernard Levin, *A World Elsewhere,* Jonathan Cape,
London, 1994, p. 43.
14. Levin, *A World Elsewhere,* p. 43.
15. See Stephen H. Webb, *American Providence: A Nation with
a Mission,* Continuum 2004, p. 34.
16. Jefferson published an edition of the New Testament in which
all references to Christ's miraculous powers were deleted so
that Jesus appeared as just one more sage. See Stephen H.
Webb, *American Providence,* p. 38.
17. In his second inaugural address Lincoln interpreted the Civil
War as a judgement of God on both sides of the conflict. See
Stephen H. Webb, *American Providence,* p. 33. In the twentieth century the influential theologian Reinhold Niebuhr (born
1892), proved a powerful critic of the notion of 'national
innocence', which he regarded as a delusion. 'America had
killed red men, enslaved black men and later on imported
yellow men for hard labour. Not much of a background for
national innocence.' Part of an article by Arthur Schlesinger
Jr, 'Forgetting Reinhold Niebuhr', *The New York Times,* 18

September 2005. Niebuhr also emphasized the mixed and ambivalent character of human nature – creative impulses matched by destructive impulses, self-regard overriding concern for others, the will to power and the constant temptation for individuals to play God to history. His thinking gave fresh impetus to the Christian doctrine of original sin and owed much to Paul, Augustine and Calvin. His major theological work was his two-volume *Nature and Destiny of Man*, first published in 1941 and 1943.

18. For the full text see www. german-lutherans-melbourne.asn. au/en/16330e-barmend.shtml

19. Paul's letter to the Galatians is the controlling text here as a sustained and passionate argument against those who were in danger of abandoning the gospel that they had received from him.

20. 'The needy shall not always be forgotten nor shall the hope of the poor perish for ever', (Ps. 9.18). In his mission to the Gentiles Paul honoured the mandate to 'remember the poor' given to him by the church leaders in Jerusalem (Gal. 2.10).

21. For all his remarkable gifts and the single-mindedness that brought him into conflict with others, Paul worked closely with his congregation and readily acknowledged his dependence on co-workers in the great cause of the kingdom. See Rom. 16.1–16.

22. Obituary, *The Economist,* 16 June 2007, p. 103.

23. See the *I Have a Dream Speech.* www.usconstitution.net/ dream.html

24. Gordon Brown, *Courage: Eight Portraits*, Bloomsbury, 2007.

25. Brown, *Courage,* p. 95.

26. Brown, *Courage,* p. 116.

Chapter 6

1. Enoch Powell rightly maintained in this respect that 'the good news of the gospel is imparted to the individual only as a member of a society . . . The most fundamental heresy of all is to imagine that the gospel is given to individuals or received by individuals or apprehended by individuals.' Cited in J. Enoch Powell, *Wrestling with the Angel*, London, 1977, p. 28.

2. Decency is an important and interesting value that is explored from a political angle in *The Politics of Decency* by Hazel

Blears MP, pamphlet published by Mutuo (September 2004). On p. 12 she writes: 'Decency is based on ideals that we are responsible for each other's health and well being, that our neighbours are joined to us by more than geography, that the benefits of society have to be repaid through obligations to society, that we need to take long term views about our actions, and we have a collective responsibility for our own property, others' property, our own children and the children of others, public spaces and the wider environment.'

3. The term 'Family of nations' seems increasingly apposite as a way of describing a world 'in which the traditional boundaries of time and space that have separated peoples, cultures, countries and cultures are rapidly disintegrating. We have the power, authority and responsibility to participate in the current political and social discourses that continue to shape the face of globalization in our world.' See Rebecca Todd Peters, *In Search of the Good Life: The Ethics of Globalization*, New York, Continuum International Publishing Group, 2004, p. 4.

4. See Encyclical Letter *Centesimus Annus,* by Pope John Paul 11 on the Hundredth Anniversary of *Rerum Novarum*, Catholic Truth Society, 1991, p. 10.

5. Lodged with personal and family papers in the Richard Nixon Library and Birthplace, Yorba Linda, California.

6. Cited in Jonathan Aitken, *Nixon: A Life*, Weidenfeld and Nicolson London, 1993, p. 58.

7. Aitken, *Nixon*, p. 461.

8. *The Ballad of Sir Andrew Barton*, cited in The Aitken Collection of Transcripts and Interviews.

9. Aitken, *Nixon*, p. 565.

10. Aitken, *Nixon*, p. 575.

11. The full quotation reads: 'From the crooked timber of humanity, no straight thing was ever made.' Cited by Immanuel Kant in *Gesammelte Schriften*, vol. 8, p. 23.

12. Brown, *Courage*, p. 243.

13. Shirley Williams, *God and Caesar: Personal Reflections on Politics and Religion*, Continuum, London, New York 2003, p. 73.

14. Williams, *God and Caesar*, p. 140. The lecture was entitled 'The Struggle for the Soul of the 21st Century.'

15. John Macmurray's description of the State has some relevance here: 'If we track the State to its lair, what shall we find? Merely a collection of overworked and worried gentle-

[handwritten annotation: I was just on the link. Dr Wasilewski at W.G.S.]

Notes

men (sic), not at all unlike ourselves, doing their best to keep the machinery of government working as well as may be, and hard put to it to keep up appearances.' See his *Persons in Relation*, Oxford Clarendon Press, 1961, p. 200.

16. See Richard Cockett, 'Leap of Faith' in *Prospect*, July 2007, Issue 136, p. 33.
17. John Macmurray wrote that 'we need one another to be ourselves'. See Blears, *The Politics of Decency*, p. 10.
18. Williams, *God and Caesar*, p. 71.
19. Garry Wills, *Saint Augustine*, Weidenfeld and Nicolson, 1999, p. 116.
20. Wills, *Saint Augustine*, p. 121.
21. See my earlier book *Facing The City*, Epworth, 2004, in particular Ch. 2 for an account of how the Church of England responded to the crisis of the cities during the Thatcher years.
22. For a fascinating and important essay on the limits, dangers and possibilities of political/religious idealism see John Gray, *Black Mass: Apocalyptic Religion and the Death of Utopia*, Penguin Allen Lane, 2007.
23. See Gray, *Black Mass*, for an interesting summary of Augustine's teaching on utopian thinking and the categorical distinction between the earthly city and the city of God, pp. 8–9.

Chapter 7

1. William Wordsworth, 'Personal Talk' cited in *The New Oxford Book of English Verse 1250–1950*, OUP, 1992, p. 507. Chosen and edited by Helen Gardner.
2. See Sigmund Freud, *The Future of an Illusion*, Hogarth Press, 1928, for his analysis of the religious impulse.
3. Quoted by H.A. Williams in *True Resurrection*, Mitchell Beazley, 1972, p. 178.
4. See John Bowker, *The Meanings of Death*, Cambridge, 1991, for an account of how the origin of religion amounts to more than a denial of death through the offer of eternal life.
5. Canon of St Paul's Cathedral and joint founder of the Christian Social Union (1889) that engaged with the social issues of the day including poverty, bad housing and sweatshop industries.
6. Francis Bacon (1561–1626), Essayist and Philosopher. Quota-

tion cited in *The Oxford Dictionary of Quotations*, Oxford University Press, 1980, p. 26.
7. Cited in Frances Spalding, *Stevie Smith: A Biography*, W.W. Norton & Company, 1989, p. 301. *Collected Poems of Stevie Smith*, New Directions Publishing Corp. Permission applied for.
8. Spalding, *Stevie Smith*, p. 242.
9. *Essays of William Hazlitt*, George Harrap & Co. Ltd., 1920, p. 163.
10. *Collins Albatross Book of Verse*, Collins, 1972, pp. 631–32 and The Marvell Press. Permission applied for.
11. From the first verse of 'Aubade', cited in Andrew Motion, *Philip Larkin: A Writer's Life*, Farrer Strauss Giraux, New York, 1993, p. 449. Philip Larkin, *Collected Poems*, Faber & Faber, 2003. Permission applied for.
12. Motion, *Philip Larkin*, p. 520
13. Motion, *Philip Larkin*, p. 372. Philip Larkin, *Collected Poems*, Faber & Faber, 2003. Permission applied for.
14. Part of a prayer from the late Evening service of Compline.
15. Blaise Pascal, *Pensées*, London, 1995, p. 34.
16. Terry Eagleton, *After Theory*, Penguin, 2004, p. 211.

Chapter 8

1. Miguel de Cervantes Saavedra (1547–1616), Spanish novelist and dramatist. His masterpiece *Don Quixote* was first published in 1605.
2. Gershem Scholem, *Kabbalah*, Jerusalem, 1974.
3. Gay Sussex, *Longsight past and present*, Manchester Free Press, 1983, pp. 12–13.
4. Sussex, *Longsight*, p. 20.
5. Sussex, *Longsight*, p. 20.
6. *The New Oxford Book of English Verse*, ed. Helen Gardner, OUP, 1992, pp. 361–62.
7. *The New English Hymnal*, Canterbury Press Norwich, 1992, No. 392.
8. Malcolm Muggeridge, *Like It Was: A Selection from the Diaries of Malcolm Muggeridge*, Collins, 1981.
9. Letter to Mlle de Chantepie, June 1857, cited by Alberto Manguel in *A History of Reading*, Flamingo, HarperCollins 1997, p. 1.
10. Manguel, *A History of Reading*, p. 44.

11. Derek Wilson, *Out of the Storm: The Life and Legacy of Martin Luther*, Hutchinson, London, 2007, p. 97.
12. Stanley Ayling, *John Wesley*, Collins, 1979, p. 93.
13. Preface to Barth's *Epistle to the Romans*, Oxford University Press, 1933, p. 1.
14. Words of the Roman Catholic theologian Karl Adam cited in William Nicholls, *The Pelican Guide to Modern Theology, Volume 1: Systematic and Philosophical Theology*, Penguin Books, 1969, p. 75.
15. R.S. Pine-Coffin (trans.), *Augustine, Confessions*, London, Penguin, 1961, Book X, Chapters 6, 8, pp. 211–13, 215–16.
16. Stanley Ayling, *John Wesley*, p. 171.
17. John Webster, 'Introducing Barth' in his *The Cambridge Companion to Karl Barth*, Cambridge University Press, 2000, p. 8.
18. W. Ritschl , 'How to Be Most Grateful to Karl Barth without Remaining a Barthian' in D. McKim (ed.), *How Karl Barth Changed My Mind*, Grand Rapids: Eerdmans, 1986, p. 87.
19. See Elaine Graham, Heather Walton and Frances Ward (eds.), *Theological Reflection: Methods*, SCM Press, 2005, p. 95.
20. See John Webster, *The Cambridge Companion to Karl Barth*, p. 300.
21. Margaret Atwood, *Negotiating with the Dead: A Writer on Writing*, Cambridge University Press, 2002.
22. See Michael Frayn, *The Human Touch: Our Part in the Creation of a Universe*, Faber & Faber, 2006, pp. 273–97. A fascinating discussion of how language helps us to 'catch hold' of things.
23. R.S. Pine-Coffin, *Augustine, Confessions*, Book 6. ch.3 p. 4.
24. Graham, Walton & Ward, *Theological Reflection: Methods*, p. 60.
25. J. Bunyan, *The Author's Apology for his Fable*, cited in Graham, Walton & Ward, *Theological Reflection: Methods*, p. 60.

Chapter 9

1. *Like It Was: The Diaries of Malcolm Muggeridge*, selected and edited by John Bright-Holmes, Collins, 1981, p. 457.
2. Richard Ingrams, *Muggeridge: The Biography*, HarperCollins, 1995, p. 247.

3. *Church Times,* 9 November 2007.
4. Malcolm Muggeridge, *Jesus Rediscovered,* Fontana, 1969, p. 11.
5. Muggeridge, *Jesus Rediscovered,* p. 10.
6. Muggeridge, *Jesus Rediscovered,* p. 34.
7. Iris Murdoch, *Existentialists and Mystics: Writings on Philosophy and Literature,* Chatto & Windus, London, 1997, p. 344.
8. *The Truth Seeking Heart: Austin Farrer and His Writings,* Canterbury Press, 2006, p. 187. Edited and introduced by Ann Loades and Robert MacSwain.
9. Richard Ingrams, *Muggeridge,* p. 13.
10. Richard Ingrams, *Muggeridge,* p. 212.
11. Richard Ingrams, *Muggeridge,* p. 250.
12. Richard Ingrams, *Muggeridge,* p. 18.
13. From the third-century hymn 'Hail Gladdening Light'.
14. Prayer from the *Gelasian Sacramentary,* (eighth century).
15. A.R. Vidler, *A Variety of Catholic Modernists,* Cambridge University Press, 1970.
16. *The Mystical Element of Religion as studied in Saint Catherine of Genoa and her Friends,* London, 1908.
17. Cited in Bernard Holland, *Selected Letters of Baron von Hügel: Edited with a Memoir,* London: J.M. Dent, 1927, p. 35.
18. Holland, *Selected Letters,* p. 35.
19. Richard Ingrams, *Muggeridge,* p. 81.
20. Iris Murdoch, *Existentialists and Mystics,* p. 344.
21. Maria Boulding, *The Coming of God,* SPCK, 1982.
22. Maria Boulding, *The Coming of God,* pp. 134–35, New edition, 1994.
23. Simone Weil, *Waiting on God,* Collins, Fontana, 1963, pp. 91–2.
24. Iris Murdoch, *Existentialists and Mystics,* p. 342.
25. Iris Murdoch, *Existentialists and Mystics,* p. 385.

Select Bibliography

Aitken, J., *Nixon: A Life,* Weidenfeld and Nicolson, London, 1993.

Atwood, M., *Negotiating with the Dead: A Writer on Writing,* Cambridge University Press, 2002.

Ayling, S., *John Wesley,* Collins, 1979.

Bainton, R., *Here I Stand,* Nashville, 1950.

Barth, K., *Epistle to the Romans,* Oxford University Press, 1933.

Blears, H., *The Politics of Decency,* Mutuo, 2004.

Bloom, H., *Where Shall Wisdom be Found?,* Ravenhead Books, 2004.

Boulding, M., *The Coming of God,* SPCK, New Edition, 1994.

Bowker, J., *The Meanings of Death,* Cambridge, 1991.

Breazeale, D. (ed. and trans.), 'On Truth and Lies in a Nonmoral Sense', in *Philosophy and Truth: Selections from Nietzsche's Notebooks of the Early 1870s,* Atlantic Highlands, N.J.: Humanities Press International, 1979.

Bridge, A., *One Man's Advent,* Collins Fount, 1985.

Bright-Holmes, J. (ed. and selected by), *Like It Was: The Diaries of Malcolm Muggeridge,* Collins, 1981.

Brontë, E., 'Last Lines' in *Best Loved Poems,* N. Philip (ed.), Little, Brown, 2000.

Brown, G., *Courage: Eight Portraits,* Bloomsbury, 2007.

Butter, P. (ed.), *William Blake,* Everyman Paperbacks, 1996.

Camus, A., *The Plague,* Penguin Modern Classics, 1977.

Cockett, R., 'Leap of Faith', in *Prospect,* Issue 136, July 2007.

Collins Albatross Book of Verse, Collins, 1972.

Davies, B., *The Thought of Thomas Aquinas,* Clarendon Press Oxford, 1993.

Dawkins, R., *The God Delusion,* Transworld, Bantam Press, 2006.

de Lubac, H., *Paradoxes of Faith*, San Francisco, Ignatius Press, 1987.

Dillard, A., *Pilgrim at Tinker Creek*, Jonathan Cape, 1975.

Dix, D.G., *The Shape of The Liturgy*, Dacre Press, A&C Black, 1945.

Dostoevsky, F., *The Brothers Karamazov*, Heinemann, 1948.

Eagleton, T., *After Theory*, Penguin, 2004.

Ecclestone, A., *A Staircase for Silence*, Darton, Longman and Todd, 1977.

Encyclical Letter *Centesimus Annus* by Pope John Paul II on the Hundredth Anniversary of *Rerum Novarum*, Catholic Truth Society, 1991.

Essays of William Hazlitt, George Harrap & Co Ltd., 1920.

Farrer, A., *Saving Belief*, Hodder & Stoughton, 1967.

Farrer, A., *The End of Man*, SPCK, 1973.

Frayn, M., *The Human Touch: Our Part in the Creation of a Universe*, Faber & Faber, 2006.

Freud, S., *The Future of an Illusion*, Hogarth Press, 1928.

Garner, R., *Facing The City: Urban Mission in the 21st Century*, Epworth Press, 2004.

Gibbon, E., *The Decline and Fall of the Roman Empire*, Lentin A., Norman B. (eds.), BCA Wordsworth Edition Ltd., 1998.

Gorringe, T., *God's Theatre: A Theology of Providence*, SCM Press, 1991.

Graham, E., Walton, H., & Ward, F. (eds.), *Theological Reflection: Methods*, SCM Press, 2005.

Gray, J., *Black Mass: Apocalyptic Religion and the Death of Utopia*, Penguin Allen Lane, 2007.

Hick, J., *Faith and Knowledge*, Fontana, 1974.

Holland, B., *Selected Letters of Baron Von Hügel: Edited with a Memoir,* London: J.M. Dent, 1927.

Houlden, J.L., *Paul's Letters from Prison*, SCM Press, 1977.

Hughes, R.T., *How Christian Faith can Sustain the Life of the Mind,* Eerdmans, 2001.

Ingrams, R., *Muggeridge: The Biography*, HarperCollins, 1995.

Johnson, S., *Rambler*, No 85 in Johnson's *Works*, Oxford, 1825.

Select Bibliography

Kafka, F., *Metamorphosis and Other Stories*, Penguin Modern Classics, 2007.

Kelly, J.N.D., *Early Christian Doctrines*, A & C Black, 1977, 5th edition.

Kelly, J.N.D., *Early Christian Creeds*, Longman, 1972, 3rd edition.

Keynes, R., *Annie's Box: Charles Darwin, His daughter and Human Evolution*, HarperCollins, 2001.

Kierkegaard, S., *Purity of Heart is to Will One Thing*, Fontana, 1961.

Knowles, D., *City of God*, Penguin Pelican, 1972.

Levin, B., *A World Elsewhere*, Jonathan Cape, London, 1994.

Llewelyn, R., *With Pity Not With Blame*, Darton, Longman & Todd, 1982.

Loades, A., & MacSwain, R. (eds.), *The Truth Seeking Heart: Austin Farrer and His Writings*, Canterbury Press 2006.

McGrath, A., *The Christian Theology Reader*, Blackwell, 1995.

MacCulloch, D., *Reformation: Europe's House Divided 1490–1700*, Allen Lane, 2003.

MacMullen, R., *Voting about God in Early Church Councils*, Yale University Press, 2006.

MacMurray, J., *Persons in Relation*, Oxford Clarendon Press, 1961.

Maitland, S., *A Big-Enough God*, Mowbray, 1995.

Manguel, A., *A History of Reading*, Flamingo, HarperCollins, 1997.

Mayne, M., *This Sunrise of Wonder*, Fount, 1995.

Moltmann, J., *The Crucified God*, SCM Press, 1974.

Motion, A., *Philip Larkin: A Writer's Life*, Farrer Strauss Giraux, New York, 1993.

Muggeridge, M., *Like It Was: A Selection from the Diaries of Malcolm Muggeridge*, Collins, 1981.

Muggeridge, M., *Jesus Rediscovered*, Fontana, 1969.

Murdoch, I., *Existentialists and Mystics: Writings on Philosophy and Literature*, Chatto & Windus, London, 1997.

Nasr, V., *The Shia Revival: How Conflicts within Islam Will Shape the Future*, Norton & Company, 2007.

Newman, J.H. (ed.), J. Coulson, *On Consulting the Faithful In Matters of Doctrine*, Collins Flame Classics, 1986.

Newman, J.H., *Idea of a University*, cited by Van de Weyer, R., and Saunders P., in *I Step, I Mount: The Vision of John Henry Newman*, Marshall Morgan and Scott, Lamp Press, 1989.

Nicholls, W., *The Pelican Guide to Modern Theology, Volume 1: Systematic and Philosophical Theology*, Penguin Books, 1969.

Otto, R., *The Idea of The Holy*, first published 1917.

Page, N. (ed.), *Thomas Hardy: Everyman's Poetry*, J.M. Dent, Everyman, 1998.

Pascal, B., *Pensées*, London, 1995.

Pine-Coffin, R.S. (trans.), *Augustine, Confessions*, London, Penguin, 1961.

Powell, E., *Wrestling with the Angel*, London, 1977.

Reynolds, D.S. (ed.), *A Historical Guide to Walt Whitman*, New York, OUP, 2000.

Ritschl, W., 'How to be Most Grateful to Karl Barth without Remaining a Barthian', in D. McKim (ed.), *How Karl Barth Changed My Mind*, Grand Rapids, Eerdmans, 1986.

Rorty R., *Philosophy and the Mirror of Nature*, Princeton University Press, 1979.

Rorty, R., *Consequences of Pragmatism*, University of Minnesota Press, 1982.

Russell, B., *History of Western Philosophy*, Routledge Classics, 2004.

Sanders, E.P., *Paul, the Law and the Jewish People*, SCM Press, 1985.

Scholem, G., *Kabbalah*, Jerusalem, 1974.

Schopenhauer, A., *The World as Will and Representation*, 1819.

Shanks, A., *Faith in Honesty: The Essential Nature of Theology*, Ashgate, 2005.

Smiley, J., *Thirteen Ways of Looking at the Novel*, Faber & Faber, 2005.

Somerset Maugham, W., *The Summing Up*, Penguin, 1971.

Spalding, F., *Stevie Smith: A Biography*, W.W. Norton & Company, 1989.

Stangroom, J. & Garvey, J. (eds.), *The Great Philosophers*, Eagle Editions Limited, 2006.

Sussex, G., *Longsight past and present*, Manchester Free Press, 1983.

Select Bibliography

Todd Peters, R., *In Search of the Good Life: The Ethics of Globalization*, New York, Continuum International Publishing Group, 2004.

Tomalin, C., *Thomas Hardy: The Time Torn Man*, Penguin Viking, 2006.

Updike, J., *Self Consciousness*, Penguin, 1990.

Vidler, A.R., *A Variety of Catholic Modernists*, Cambridge University Press, 1970.

Vogels, H.J. (ed.), *Florilegium Patristicum*, vol. 29, Bonn: Peter Honstein, 1930.

Watson, P., *A Terrible Beauty: a History of the People and Ideas that Shaped the Modern Mind*, Weidenfeld & Nicolson, 2000.

Webb, S.H., *American Providence: A Nation with a Mission*, Continuum, 2004.

Webster, J., 'Introducing Barth' in his *The Cambridge Companion to Karl Barth*, Cambridge University Press, 2000.

Weil, S., *Waiting on God*, Collins Fontana, 1963.

Williams, H.A., *True Resurrection*, Mitchell Beazley, 1972.

Williams, R., *Why Study the Past? The Quest for the Historical Church*, Darton, Longman & Todd, 2005.

Williams, S., *God and Caesar: Personal Reflections on Politics and Religion*, Continuum, London, New York, 2003.

Wills, G., *Saint Augustine*, Weidenfeld & Nicolson, 1999.

Wilson, B., *Decency and Disorder: The Age of Cant 1789–1837*, Faber & Faber, 2007.

Wilson, D., *Out of the Storm: The Life and Legacy of Martin Luther*, Hutchinson, 2007.

Wittgenstein, L., *Tractatus-Logico Philosophicus*, 1922, and *Philosophical Investigations*, published posthumously in 1951.

Wolpert, L., *Six Impossible Things Before Breakfast: The Evolutionary Origins of Belief*, Faber & Faber, 2005.